YouTube

DATE DUE

12-18 09 ʲ	

YouTube

Online Video and Participatory Culture

JEAN BURGESS AND JOSHUA GREEN

With contributions by

HENRY JENKINS AND JOHN HARTLEY

polity

First published in 2009 by Polity Press

Polity Press
65 Bridge Street
Cambridge CB2 1UR, UK

Polity Press
350 Main Street
Malden, MA 02148, USA

ISBN-13: 978-0-7456-4478-3
ISBN-13: 978-0-7456-4479-0 (pb)

A catalogue record for this book is available from the British Library.

Typeset in 10.25 on 13 pt FF Scala
by Servis Filmsetting Ltd, Stockport, Cheshire
Printed and bound in the United States by Maple-Vail

The publisher has used its best endeavours to ensure that the URLs for external websites referred to in this book are correct and active at the time of going to press. However, the publisher has no responsibility for the websites and can make no guarantee that a site will remain live or that the content is or will remain appropriate.

Every effort has been made to trace all copyright holders, but if any have been inadvertently overlooked the publishers will be pleased to include any necessary credits in any subsequent reprint or edition.

For further information on Polity, visit our website: www.politybooks.com

Contents

Preface

Love it or loathe it, YouTube is now part of the mainstream media landscape, and a force to be reckoned with in contemporary popular culture. Although it isn't the only video-sharing website on the Internet, YouTube's rapid rise, diverse range of content, and public prominence in the Western, English-speaking world make it useful for understanding the evolving relationships between new media technologies, the creative industries, and the politics of popular culture. The aim of this book is to work through some of the often competing ideas about just what YouTube is, and what it might or might not turn out to be for.

The site's value – what YouTube has turned out to be 'for' so far – is co-created by YouTube Inc., now owned by Google, the users who upload content to the website, and the audiences who engage around that content. The contributors are a diverse group of participants – from large media producers and rights-owners such as television stations, sports companies, and major advertisers, to small-to-medium enterprises looking for cheap distribution or alternatives to mainstream broadcast systems, cultural institutions, artists, activists, media literate fans, non-professional and amateur media producers. Each of these participants approaches YouTube with their own purposes and aims and collectively shape YouTube as a dynamic cultural system: YouTube is a site of participatory culture.

The fact that YouTube is co-created is not always apparent to either YouTube Inc. or the participants within the system. Indeed, as we argue throughout, many of these different participants engage with YouTube as if it is a space specifically designed for them and that should therefore serve their own particular interests, often without an appreciation of the roles played by others. This is the source of the many ongoing conflicts around the way that YouTube as a site of participatory culture should develop.

In the chapters that follow, we begin by looking at YouTube's origins and the prehistory of the debates around it, contextualizing them within the politics of popular culture, especially in relation to the emergence of new media. Drawing on a survey of the website's most popular content, we uncover some of the ways YouTube has been put to use, deploying this discussion to think through the implications of the practices of cultural participation that take place there, and their relationship to long-running debates about the place of media in everyday life.

Moving beyond the affordances of digital technologies and their potential to enable active cultural participation, YouTube also presents us with an opportunity to confront some of participatory culture's most pressing problems: the unevenness of participation and voice; the apparent tensions between commercial interests and the public good; and the contestation of ethics and social norms that occurs as belief systems, interests, and cultural differences collide. In the later chapters we focus on some of the most important new debates around the creative industries, the new media, and the new economy: user-led innovation, amateur production, and questions of labour; the apparent tensions between global connectedness and commercial monopolies; and definitions of new media literacy.

At the conclusion of the book are two specially commissioned essays, one by Henry Jenkins and one by John Hartley. They look outward from our detailed study of YouTube, which is grounded in the contemporary moment, to provide more expansive explorations of the challenges and opportunities developments like YouTube represent to some of the central areas of concern in media and cultural studies, past, present, and future. Jenkins asks us to remember the often under-acknowledged prehistories of YouTube that are to be found in minority, activist, and alternative media, in order better to understand the potential and limits of YouTube to support cultural diversity. John Hartley's concluding chapter casts an even wider net, situating YouTube within the *longue durée* history of media, popular literacy, and the public. It addresses the question of the extent to which user-created, self-mediated expression is capable of being 'scaled up' to contribute to a more inclusive cultural public sphere and the growth of knowledge.

Acknowledgments

It is common practice these days to acknowledge that academic books are produced out of collective rather than individual effort, but in this case it is especially true. This book is not only the result of a collaboration between authors; it is also the outcome of a longstanding and fruitful partnership between two institutions on opposite sides of the planet – Queensland University of Technology in Brisbane, and Massachusetts Institute of Technology in Boston. The research project that informed this book was supported by the ARC Centre of Excellence for Creative Industries and Innovation and the Creative Industries Faculty at QUT, and the Program in Comparative Media Studies (CMS) at MIT. Additionally, some of the data we draw on throughout this book were collected as part of a project completed by the Convergence Culture Consortium. The Consortium is a partnership between CMS and MTV Networks, Yahoo!, Turner Broadcasting, Fidelity Investments, and GSD&M Idea City.

We need to offer special thanks to the diligent coders who worked on gathering data with us: Sam Ford, Eleanor Baird, Lauren Silberman, Xiaochang Li, Ana Domb Krauskopf, and Eli Koger. We are grateful to them not only for their hard work but also for their intellectual engagement and spirited contributions to the project. We thank Rik Eberhardt at CMS for his help collecting and managing the data; Jenny Burton for last-minute editorial assistance; and Paul Brand for his research assistance as part of a QUT Creative Industries Faculty Vacation Research Experience Scholarship.

At Polity, we are grateful to our commissioning editor John Thompson for originally championing this project, to Andrea

Drugan for supporting it as part of the Digital Media & Society series, and to Sarah Lambert for her assistance with the process. We would also like to express our thanks to the anonymous reviewers for their robust and valuable comments and suggestions.

Colleagues at our home institutions and around the world provided feedback, resources, difficult questions, or moral support: our thanks go to John Banks, Trine Bjørkmann Berry, Sarah Brouillette, Kate Crawford, Stuart Cunningham, Mark Deuze, Sam Ford, Anne Galloway, Melissa Gregg, Gerard Goggin, Jonathan Gray, Greg Hearn, Helen Klaebe, Kylie Jarrett, Robert Kozinets, Patricia Lange, Jason Potts, Alice Robison, Christina Spurgeon, and Graeme Turner.

Finally, we owe much to our co-authors and mentors Henry Jenkins and John Hartley, who have not only generously committed some of their ideas and energies to this book, but who have also encouraged and supported us to pursue the research collaboration of which this is the outcome.

Josh would like to thank his parents, his friends, and Allison Perlman for their support, and for forgiving his absences. Jean would like to thank her parents, her friends, and Julie Woodward for their steadfast support, and for not asking "How's the book going?" more often than could be helped.

CHAPTER ONE

How YouTube Matters

Founded by Chad Hurley, Steve Chen, and Jawed Karim, former employees of online commerce website PayPal, YouTube's website was officially launched with little public fanfare in June 2005. The original innovation was a technological (but non-unique) one: YouTube was one of a number of competing services aiming to remove the technical barriers to the widespread sharing of video online. The website provided a very simple, integrated interface within which users could upload, publish, and view streaming videos without high levels of technical knowledge, and within the technological constraints of standard browser software and relatively modest bandwidth. YouTube set no limits on the number of videos users could upload, offered basic community functions such as the opportunity to link to other users as friends, and provided URLs and HTML code that enabled videos to be easily embedded into other websites, a feature that capitalized on the recent introduction of popularly accessible blogging technologies. With the exception of a limit on the duration of videos that could be uploaded, YouTube's offerings were comparable to other online video start-ups at the time.[1]

Most versions of YouTube's history conform to the Silicon Valley myth of the garage entrepreneur, where technological and business innovation comes from youthful visionaries working outside of established enterprises; where, out of humble origins in an office over a pizzeria with a paper sign on the door (Allison, 2006), a multi-billion dollar success story emerges. In this story, the moment of success arrived in October 2006, when Google acquired YouTube for $1.65 billion.[2] By November 2007 it was the most popular entertainment website in Britain, with the BBC website in second place,[3] and in early 2008 it was, according to various web metrics services, consistently in the top ten most visited websites globally.[4] As of April 2008, YouTube hosted upwards of 85 million videos, a number that represents a tenfold increase over the previous year and that continues to increase exponentially.[5] Internet market research company com-Score reported that the service accounted for 37 percent of all Internet videos watched inside the United States, with the next largest service, Fox Interactive Media, accounting for only 4.2 percent.[6] As a user-created content community, its sheer size and mainstream popularity were unprecedented.

How did this happen? There are three different myths about the emergence of YouTube into mainstream popularity. According to the tech community, the rise of YouTube can be traced to a profile of the site written by prominent technology-business blog TechCrunch on 8 August 2005 (Arrington, 2005a), which itself made the front page of Slashdot, an agenda-setting user-driven technology news site.[7] The 'news for nerds' site was prompt both to critique YouTube's technological architecture and add YouTube to their roster of sites to watch.

As told by Jawed Karim, the third co-founder who left the business to return to college in November 2005, the success of the site is due to the implementation of four key features – video recommendations via the 'related videos' list, an email link to enable video sharing, comments (and other social networking functionality), and an embeddable video player (Gannes, 2006). These features were implemented as part of a redesign after the failure of previous attempts to popularize the website, attempts that included offering $100 to attractive girls who posted ten or more videos. According to Karim, the founders reportedly didn't receive a single reply to this offer, which they posted on Craigslist (Gannes, 2006).[8]

The third narrative of YouTube's success relates to a satirical sketch from *Saturday Night Live* featuring two nerdy, stereotypical New Yorkers rapping about buying cupcakes and going to see the *Chronicles of Narnia*. In December 2005 this clip – entitled 'Lazy Sunday' – became something of a break-out YouTube hit.

The two-and-a-half-minute sketch was viewed 1.2 million times in its first ten days online and had been seen more than five million times by February 2006, when NBC Universal demanded YouTube remove it, along with 500 other clips, or face legal action under the Digital Millennium Copyright Act (Biggs, 2006). The rise and fall of 'Lazy Sunday' brought YouTube to the notice of the popular press as something other than a technological development. For *The New York Times* (Biggs, 2006), 'Lazy Sunday' demonstrated the potential of YouTube as an outlet for established media to reach out to the elusive but much-desired youth audience. As much as a viral marketing wonderland, however, the site was reported as a looming threat to the established logics of the broadcast landscape (Kerwin, 2006; Wallenstein, 2006a). Although early reporting in the features, technology, and business pages discussed YouTube and video sharing as the Internet's new 'new thing' (Byrne, 2005; Graham, 2005; Kirsner, 2005; Nussenbaum, Ryan, and Lewis, 2005; Rowan, 2005) it was through this 'big media'-related event that YouTube became a regular *subject* for the mainstream media.

Each of these narratives created a different idea of what YouTube was: was it another online fad, beloved by the tech crowd? A clever invention that people needed to be convinced to use? Or a media distribution platform, kind of like television? While attention from early adopters and the mainstream press certainly moved the service forward, YouTube's ascendancy has occurred amid a fog of uncertainty and contradiction around what it is actually *for*. YouTube's apparent or stated mission has continuously morphed as a result of both corporate practices and audience use. In August 2005, only a few months into the life of the service, the 'About Us' page offered only the most tentative and vague hints at the possible uses of YouTube:

> Show off your favorite videos to the world
> Take videos of your dogs, cats, and other pets
> Blog the videos you take with your digital camera or cell phone
> Securely and privately show videos to your friends and family
>   around the world
> . . . and much, much more!

In these early days, the website carried the byline 'Your Digital Video Repository,' a statement which conflicts somewhat with the now-notorious exhortation to 'Broadcast Yourself.' This shift from the idea of the website as a personal storage facility for video content to a platform for public self-expression matches YouTube to the ideas about a user-led revolution that characterizes rhetoric around 'Web 2.0' (Grossman, 2006b). Despite the insistence that the service was designed for sharing personal videos among existing social networks (even, as above, explicitly referring to the paradigmatic amateur video genre – the cat video), it was a combination of the mass popularity of particular user-created videos and the uses of YouTube to distribute broadcast media content that captured the public imagination. It is also this combination that has positioned it as a key place where disputes over copyright, participatory culture, and the market structures of online video distribution are taking place.

As a media company, YouTube is a platform for, and an aggregator of, content, but it is not a content producer itself. It is an example of what David Weinberger (2007) calls 'meta businesses' – the 'new category of business that enhances the value of information developed elsewhere and thus benefits the original creators of that information' (224). Weinberger's examples include Apple's iTunes store, which profits through music purchases but doesn't 'provide' music in the way that record labels do – bearing the costs of discovery and production; rather, iTunes makes aggregated information about music 'more searchable, more findable, and more usable' (225). So too, YouTube serves a discovery role for video producers, drawing attention to content, as well as offering revenue streams from advertising sold on the website.

Similarly, YouTube is not actually in the video business – its business, rather, is the provision of a convenient and usable platform for online video *sharing*: users (some of them premium content partners) supply the content, which in turn brings new participants and new audiences. To a certain extent then, YouTube is in the reach business as understood in traditional media business models; supporting a high volume of visitors and a range of different audiences, it offers participants a way to garner wide exposure. But Karim's proposition that the website's success can be traced to four key features that enabled media sharing reveals the most about the success behind the service. While it would eventually seek premium content distribution deals and, once utilized, a tiered access program that provided paying users with the ability to upload longer videos, YouTube has always oriented its services toward content *sharing*, including the sharing of mundane and amateur content, rather than the provision of high-quality video.[9]

YouTube's business practices have proven particularly controversial, both with the old media and with some of the most active members of YouTube's social network. While some Big Content players – large media producers and rights holders such as the Warner and Universal Music Groups – have signed revenue sharing deals with YouTube,[10] others such as US conglomerate Viacom have rejected these deals, arguing that the service induces and profits from copyright infringement (Helft, 2008). Many of these companies seem uncomfortable with their role as participants in a space where they don't exercise complete control over the distribution and circulation of their cultural products. At the same time, some of the most active members of the YouTube social network have expressed discomfort with the interjection of corporate players into a space they experience as community generated.

The discomfort of both corporate interests and community participants points to the uncertainty associated with the meaning and uses of YouTube. This uncertainty can also be interpreted as the source of YouTube's cultural 'generativity' (Zittrain, 2008), which emerges from its multiple roles as a high-volume website, a broadcast platform, a media archive, and a social network. YouTube's value is not produced solely or even predominantly by the top-down activities of YouTube, Inc. as a company. Rather, various forms of cultural, social, and economic values are collectively produced by users *en masse*, via their consumption, evaluation, and entrepreneurial activities. Consumer co-creation (Potts *et al.*, 2008b) is fundamental to

YouTube's value proposition as well as to its disruptive influence on established media business models. When we think in this way, we can begin to think about how YouTube matters in terms of culture. For YouTube, participatory culture is not a gimmick or a sideshow; it is absolutely core business.

Making Sense of YouTube

At the heart of this book is an attempt to treat YouTube in itself as an object of research. Writing about the methodological challenges of making sense of television nearly two decades ago, Stephen Heath described it as:

> a somewhat difficult object, unstable, all over the place, tending derisively to escape anything we say about it: given the speed of its changes (in technology, economics, programming), its interminable flow (of images and sounds, their endlessly disappearing present), its quantitative everydayness (the very quality of this medium each and every day). (Heath, 1990: 267)

YouTube, even more than television, is a particularly unstable object of study, marked by dynamic change (both in terms of videos and organization), a diversity of content (which moves with a different rhythm to television but likewise flows through, and often disappears from, the service), and a similar quotidian frequency, or 'everydayness.' It is further complicated by its double function as both a 'top-down' platform for the distribution of popular culture and a 'bottom-up' platform for vernacular creativity. It is variously understood as a distribution platform that can make the products of commercial media widely popular, challenging the promotional reach the mass media is accustomed to monopolizing, while at the same time a platform for user-created content where challenges to commercial popular culture might emerge, be they user-created news services, or generic forms such as vlogging – which might in turn be appropriated and exploited by the traditional media industry. Because there is not yet a shared understanding of YouTube's common culture, each scholarly approach to understanding how YouTube works must make choices among these interpretations, in effect recreating it as a different object each time – at this early stage of research, each study of YouTube gives us a different understanding of what YouTube actually *is*.

An ambition to contribute to an understanding of how YouTube works as a site of participatory culture also requires dealing with both specificity and scale, and so presents epistemo-logical and methodological challenges to the humanities as well as to the social sciences. The methods of cultural and media stud-ies (and anthropology) are particularly adept at the close, richly contextualized analysis of the local and the specific, bringing this close analysis into dialogue with context, guided by and speaking back to cultural theory. Work based on these approaches is used throughout this book. But scale at the level which YouTube rep-resents tests the limits of the explanatory power of even our best grounded or particularist accounts. As cultural studies research-ers, if we determined at the outset we were interested in exploring remix culture, or music fandom, or foot fetish videos, or DIY cooking shows, or any number of other niche uses of YouTube, we would be sure to find sufficient examples among the more than 85 million videos (and counting) that are currently available in the YouTube archive – although, we may not find as many as we would expect. The challenge we set ourselves in this book is to get beyond the level of particular examples or themes, and to gain some perspective on YouTube as a mediated cultural system.

Perhaps unsurprisingly, approaches to YouTube that attempt to comprehend it as a system have, so far, been restricted to the 'hard' end of social science – usually, from computer science and informatics, employing methodological tools like social network analysis (Cha *et al.*, 2007; Gill *et al.*, 2007). These studies are used, for instance, to reveal content patterns, to explore the popularity life-cycles of videos across the website, and to map the behavioral patterns of users based on the traces that they leave behind.

Such approaches draw heavily on the most obvious and acces-sible features of the information architecture of the website itself, trading scale off against nuance and complexity. For example, hyperlink analysis can be used productively to map large-scale patterns in connections between videos or users, but only if those connections have been 'hard-wired' as hyperlinks. What this analysis misses are the many social connections and conflicts between participants in the YouTube community that are created via the *content* of the videos. Much of this large-scale, computer-assisted research also tends to rely on YouTube's own categorization and tagging systems, which enable uploaders to describe and sort their videos by content, theme, and style. The limited choices of categories YouTube provides, with titles such as 'Pets & Animals' and 'Cars & Vehicles,' at best offer a very general framework for organizing content across the website; and one that is imposed by design rather than emerging organically out of collective practice. They are necessarily broad and unable to contain much information about the videos themselves – they tell us little that is useful about genres, aesthetics, or the modes of communication associated with them. Similarly, the strategic use of the website's tagging functionality – where uploaders apply popular but perhaps inaccurate tags and titles to content and mark videos as responses to popular but unrelated content in order to increase the chances of a video being seen – make analyses of YouTube based primarily on those data problematic. It is naive simply to treat user-assigned tags, titles, and descriptions as matters of fact; indeed the *misuses* of tags may well turn out to be more interesting than their 'proper' uses.

At the other end of the methodological spectrum, Patricia Lange's two-year ethnography with the YouTube community has produced a number of important insights into the ways YouTube operates as a social networking site for certain participants, and the rich mundanity of the communicative practices that take place there. Most importantly, her work insistently reminds us of the need to consider fully the lived experience and materiality of everyday cultural practice.

This work is important because it asks us to think about the *uses* of YouTube by real people as part of everyday life and as part of the mix of media we all use as part of our lives, rather than thinking about YouTube as if it is a weightless depository of content. Like millions of other people, we use YouTube this way ourselves – we watch videos after we stumble across them on blogs, or click on links sent to us in emails by our friends, and we pass them along to others. We have our own YouTube channels and even occasionally upload and/or make videos to contribute to the growing archive of material available there.

But, while the book benefits greatly from the insights of ethnographic work on YouTube, we didn't do any ethnographic research ourselves. Such an investigation would have taken us in a different direction, telling us more about how YouTube works as part of the lived experience of our research participants than it would about how YouTube is structured and evolving as a media system in the economic and social context of broader media and technological change. Also, ethnographic approaches tend to emphasize the significance of the social networking aspects of YouTube, and so tend to focus on individual users who operate outside the commercial media system (see, for example, Lange, 2007a; Lange 2007b). In her work on the YouTube community, Lange (2007a) develops a typology that breaks down the notion of a singular 'casual user' and helpfully problematizes how we can understand participation in YouTube. But inevitably this typology excludes YouTube participants who might make use of the website for its promotional capacity, rather than its social networking aspects – a group that would include professional media producers and brands, both large and small.

Attempting to address the missing middle between large-scale quantitative analysis and the sensitivity of qualitative methods, we combined the close reading of media and cultural studies with a survey of 4,320 of the videos calculated to be 'most popular' on the website at a particular moment – gathered between August and November 2007. As humanities researchers, this survey of content provided a way to order a relatively large body of raw material without selecting it in advance, so that we were able to identify patterns across the sample, as well as to interrogate clusters of individual texts using our much more familiar qualitative methods. This strategy has been useful throughout this book for purposes such as identifying controversies and mapping aesthetic characteristics across particular cultural forms: it gives us some idea of the shape and scope of YouTube's 'common culture'; raising some new questions about how to think about 'the popular' in the context of participatory culture; and provides some new conceptual tools in the quest to move forward from 'ignorance to uncertainty' (Matthews, 2008).

Combining a broad survey of content and some quantitative methods with critical and qualitative modes of analysis, our study sought not only to measure the extent of popularity of particular forms and uses, but how mapping those forms and uses helps us to understand the emerging issues for the cultural politics of digital media. Moving back and forth between the empirical findings of this study, critical discussion of the current public debates, and the insights provided by existing media and cultural studies perspectives, this book places YouTube into dialogue with the central problems that cultural and media studies have been grappling with for decades, focusing on the politics of popular culture and media power. These are the questions that are encoded in the term 'participatory culture.'

YouTube as a Site of Participatory Culture

Participatory culture is a term that is often used to talk about the apparent link between more accessible digital technologies, user-created content, and some kind of shift in the power relations between media industries and their consumers (see especially Jenkins, 2006a). Indeed, Jenkins' definition of a 'participatory culture' is one in which 'fans and other consumers are invited to actively participate in the creation and circulation of new content' (Jenkins, 2006a: 290). This might seem at first like a rather comfortable arrangement (and one which Jenkins presents as a potential rather than present reality), but YouTube proves that in practice the economic and cultural rearrangements that 'participatory culture' stands for are as disruptive and uncomfortable as they might be potentially liberating. The debates and struggles around YouTube as a site of participatory culture that we discuss in the following chapter are less about technology and more about cultural and political questions: who gets to speak, and who gets the attention; what compensations or rewards there are for creativity and work; and the uncertainties around various forms of expertise and authority. These are all questions that have come up time and again in debates about the value and legitimacy of popular culture, especially when new forms of it emerge, and particularly (as with YouTube) when those new forms are made accessible via mass media technologies.

These questions about popular culture – the culture of 'the people' – have a very long history in Cultural Studies and the disciplines which preceded it (see Storey, 2003). Struggles over the meaning and value of popular culture are symptoms of modernity, tied up with shifting class politics, the mass industrialization of cultural production, and the 'common' people's growing affluence and access to education. For cultural studies theorists at various times, culture is both 'ordinary' (Hoggart, 1957; Williams, 1958) and a potential site of symbolic struggle, empowerment, or self-expression (Fiske, 1989; 1992a). For many of these theorists, bottom-up participation and 'the popular' are rarely if ever valued for their own sake; rather they matter only insofar as they can be understood as part of a political project of emancipation and democracy, tied to the politics of class, race, and gender. This was a point made with searing clarity in Stuart Hall's famous (1981) statement that:

> Popular culture is one of the sites where this struggle for and against a culture of the powerful is engaged: it is also the stake to be won or lost in that struggle. It is the arena of consent and resistance. It is partly where hegemony arises, and where it is secured. It is not a sphere where socialism, a socialist culture – already fully formed – might be simply 'expressed'. But it is one of the places where socialism might be constituted. That is why 'popular culture' matters. Otherwise, to tell you the truth, I don't give a damn about it. (Hall, 1981: 239)

These longstanding struggles over the politics of the popular in modernity have left a legacy in the competing definitions of popular culture operating today. On the one hand, popular culture is

most commonly thought of – often pejoratively – as mass commercial, consumer culture – reality TV, shopping malls, celebrity
gossip, the Top 40, and computer games. Under this definition,
popular culture is distinct from high culture through its conditions of production and consumption within capitalism, as much
as its aesthetics and associated identities. A second way of understanding 'the culture of the people' is as authentic, homegrown
culture, part of the long traditions of folk culture, distinct from
both high culture (the Paris Opera) on the one hand, and mass
commercial culture (Paris Hilton) on the other. The residual desire
for a contemporary folk culture that underpinned the West Coast
counterculture later articulated to technoculture and US individu-
alism to produce the 'digital utopianism' (F. Turner, 2006) that
surfaces repeatedly as part of the DIY ideology of participatory
culture, the valorization of amateur and community media, and
hopeful ideas about the democratization of cultural production
(see both Benkler, 2006: 274–8; and Jenkins, 2006a: 135–7). Both
of these definitions of the popular, and the politics that go along
with them, crop up in the discourses around YouTube.

In the 1990s, fan production was mobilized as a recuperation of
both of these versions of the popular – cultural studies used it as evi-
dence that at least some of the audience – even for mass media like
commercial television – was active rather than 'passive' and simply
acted *upon* (Fiske, 1992b; Jenkins, 1992). Studies of fan cultures
proved that (some) audiences were creative, engaging in legitimate
fields of cultural production in a symbiotic (and at times uneasy)
relationship with the 'big media,' who saw themselves as the origi-
nating authors of the texts, characters, and fictional worlds that fans
'made over' for their own purposes. Underlying fan studies is a
commitment to the idea of everyday life as a site of potential creative
resistance, to a large extent appropriated from theorists of everyday
life such as Michel de Certeau (1984), and articulated to a feminist
politics of popular culture. Continuing this tradition, much work on
popular culture online to date has focused on fan communities and
their creative practices (see, for example, Hellekson and Busse, eds,
2006), and fandom is frequently represented as a site of resistance

to capitalism that is always at the same time in danger of being captured or shut down by corporate interests (Consalvo, 2003).

However, the exponential growth of more mundane and formerly private forms of 'vernacular creativity' as part of public culture (Burgess, 2007), as evident in the growth of online social networks, blogs, photosharing, and videoblogging; the incorporation of user-generated content in the logics of public service broadcasting (even in the latest BBC charter); the new business models associated with Web 2.0 relying on user-generated content and user-led innovation (O'Reilly, 2005); and the attempts of brand capitalism to manufacture bottom-up engagement through viral marketing (Spurgeon, 2008), demonstrate that there is a broader 'participatory turn' taking place, so that these two opposing definitions of the popular are converging. Everyday creativity is no longer either trivial or quaintly authentic, but instead occupies central stage in discussions of the media industries and their future in the context of digital culture (see, for example, OECD, 2007). Consumption is no longer necessarily seen as the end point in an economic chain of production but as a dynamic site of innovation and growth in itself (Bruns, 2007; Potts *et al.*, 2008b), and this extends to the practices of media consumers or audiences (see Hartley, 2004; Green and Jenkins, 2009). Further, the practices of fan communities are now increasingly incorporated within the logics of the media industries (Green and Jenkins, 2009; Jenkins, 2006b: 144–9; Johnson, 2007; Murray, 2004; Shefrin, 2004). Increasingly, more sophisticated narratives, which reward the close attention and repeated viewing associated with media fandom, are becoming more commonplace (Mittell, 2006; Jenkins 2006a), and the committed, attentive, and often productive practices of fans provide models for desired audience and consumer behavior in a wider range of industries (Gray, Sandvoss, and Harrington, 2008).

In *The Wealth of Networks*, Yochai Benkler's (2006) enthusiasm about the possibilities of the new networks of social production relies on an imagined opposition between a pre-industrial folk culture and the alienation of twentieth-century mass popular culture, which, he argues, 'displaced' folk culture and transformed individuals and communities from 'coproducers and replicators to passive consumers' (Benkler, 2006: 296). In the light of the convergence between commercial popular culture and community participation that YouTube represents, this claim that the emergence of peer-produced culture represents a renaissance of folk culture reproduces too simplistic a divide between the culture of the people and the culture of the mass media industries. YouTube is experienced in a range of different ways by consumer-citizens via a hybrid model of engagement with popular culture – part amateur production, part creative consumption. From an audience point of view, is it a platform that provides access to culture, or a platform that enables consumers to participate as producers? This openness is the source of YouTube's diversity and reach, as well as the cause of the many clashes between top-down control and bottom-up emergence that produce its politics.

YouTube has a place within the long history and uncertain future of media change, the politics of cultural participation, and the growth of knowledge. Clearly, it is both a symptom of, and an actor in, economic and cultural transitions that are tied up somehow with digital technologies, the Internet, and the more direct participation of consumers; but it is important to be careful about just what claims are made for the historical status of these transitions. Like massively multiplayer online games (MMOGs), YouTube illustrates the increasingly complex relations among producers and consumers in the creation of meaning, value, and agency. There is no doubt it is a site of cultural and economic disruption. However, these moments of media transition should not be understood as radical historical breaks, but rather as periods of increased turbulence, becoming visible as various established practices, influences, and ideas compete with emerging ones as part of the long history of culture, media, and society. YouTube represents not so much the collision as the co-evolution and uneasy co-existence of 'old' and 'new' media industries, forms, and practices.

CHAPTER TWO

YouTube and the Mainstream Media

YouTube clearly represents a disruption to existing media business models and is emerging as a new site of media power. It has received significant press attention, and is now part, however begrudgingly accepted, of the mainstream media landscape, but it is also regularly used as a vehicle for rehearsing public debates about new media and the Internet as a disruptive force on business and society, particularly with regard to young people. The assumptions underlying these representations of YouTube deserve a closer look.

In engaging with these debates, this chapter draws on a thematic analysis of mainstream media coverage of YouTube throughout 2006 and 2007. What emerges is a set of issues that, while 'newsworthy' in the traditional sense, have more to do with the news agenda of mainstream media than with the way YouTube works. It tends to be framed as either as a lawless repository for a flood of amateur content, or (in Business sections particularly) as a big player in the new economy. These definitional frames result in a steady but repetitive stream of news stories clustering around some familiar themes: youth, celebrity, and morality on the one hand; copyright law and media business on the other.

These debates, however familiar, contribute to shaping our understanding of what YouTube is and what matters about it: media discourses – whether celebratory, condemnatory, or somewhere in between – cannot help but both reflect and shape the meaning of new media forms as they evolve. Media 'framing' (De Vreese, 2005) and reality create each other, forming a dynamic feedback loop, so that the mainstream or incumbent media's struggles to comprehend and make sense of the meanings and implications of YouTube not only reflect public concerns, but also help to produce them. The repetitive framing of YouTube as an amateur 'free-for-all' rather than a place for community or artistic experimentation, for instance, situates it as a space where the public or the masses are rising up from the bottom, so that the matters of concern around it have to do with lawlessness, the crisis of expertise, and the collapse of cultural value. Similarly, mainstream media discourses about YouTube have the power to define the issues that may later be realized in policy, in law, and even in material form, so concern about 'piracy' or 'cyberbullying' can give the impression that regulatory interventions are required – like Digital Rights Management (DRM) to fight piracy, or blocking YouTube on school computers to fight cyberbullying. Our aim here is not simply to point out that mainstream media discourses about new media are wrong, but to work through them and provide some alternative perspectives that can be used in public debates or in practice.

One of the most striking things about mainstream reporting of YouTube is the degree to which these matters of concern conflict with one another. For example, on New Year's Eve 2007, Australian current affairs programs *Today Tonight* and *A Current Affair* both broadcast stories about the most popular YouTube clips of 2007, describing the website as both a repository for 'amazing, embarrassing, and sometimes downright dangerous moments' around the world, and a launching platform for 'many new stars' ('YouTube's Most Watched,' 2007; 'Best YouTube Videos,' 2007). YouTube as good object is a site of wacky, weird, and wonderful user-generated content. Within only a few weeks, however, the same programs returned to business-as-usual stories about cyberbullying on YouTube, framing it as a very bad object indeed – an under-regulated site of lawless, unethical and pathological behavior centered around youth as a risk category. But as YouTube has evolved, so has its role in the cycles of news reporting: from being described as one among a plethora of novel new media applications and a potential site of ordinary self expression, to its prominence as a threat to media dominance and civil order, and, more recently, as a bona fide mainstream, if somewhat unruly and under-regulated, medium in its own right.

Media Panics

In press coverage, YouTube is often used to express familiar anxieties about young people and digital media, especially in relation to the risks, uses and misuses of Internet and mobile phone technologies. These stories are characterized by the particularly modern convergence of 'trouble-as-fun, fun-as-trouble' Hebdige (1988: 30) saw in media images of youth in postwar Britain – where young people are represented as an exotic other, at once exuberantly creative and dangerous. Images of youth have been closely associated with ideas about shifts in capitalism and the organization of social structures such as class, wealth distribution, and consumption practices (Murdock and McCron, 1976: 10), and where new media are seen as key disruptive agents, the two are often conflated. Indeed, Kirsten Drotner (2000: 150) argues young people are connected to media by complementary metaphors of newness and change, and because of this, discourses around youth and discourses around new media inevitably become entangled. In the case of YouTube the 'trouble-as-fun, fun-as-trouble' convergence is further amplified through adult anxieties about an 'intergenerational [digital] divide' mobilized through discourses of 'technological exoticism' (Herring, 2008), where *both* YouTube and the masses of 'youth' assumed to be its default users, are undisciplined, savage, and at the same time new and exciting (Driscoll and Gregg, 2008). This is apparent even in seemingly positive arguments about young people's 'natural' technological prowess, such as Prensky's (2001a; 2001b) notion of the 'digital native.'

This equation of new media platforms like YouTube with 'youth' flows through to policy as well. In a recent attempt to encourage young people to be more physically active, the Department for Culture, Media, and Sport in the UK created a website intended to aggregate user-created content about sports performance. The idea seemed to be, "If you can't beat 'em, join 'em" – the development was reportedly motivated by the fact 'the Government can't get the YouTube generation away from their computer screens' (Eason, 2008).

Some news stories about YouTube follow the pattern of the 'moral panic' – a term which has now passed into everyday language but which in cultural studies is used to describe a specific cycle of co-influence between media representation and social reality around issues of public concern (Cohen, 1972). In the landmark cultural studies text *Policing the Crisis*, Stuart Hall *et al.* (1978) analyzed the way mugging in Britain was constructed as a new crime that represented specific threats to society in the context of a particular historical 'conjuncture', arguing the focus on this newly acute 'problem' worked to obscure what was really a crisis for institutionalized ideological power. As the police and the media targeted 'mugging,' the problem was amplified in the public imagination and in reality,[1] constituting a 'moral panic'. Similarly, in media coverage of YouTube, stories exhibiting the characteristics of a moral panic draw on and amplify two interlocking strains of public anxiety: youth and morality on the one hand, and new media and its 'effects' on the other. Drotner (1999) describes this double pattern of convergence between new media anxiety and moral anxiety as a 'media panic', and demonstrates that it has a long history as an 'intrinsic and recurrent' feature of modernity.

Tom Rawstorne and Brad Crouch's (2006) opinion piece in News Limited paper *The Sunday Mail* provides a telling example, by turns blaming and absolving both young people and YouTube for deviance. Rawstorne and Crouch (2006) paint YouTube as a video free-for-all, experiencing 'unchecked growth' where a sinister space filled with graphic content lies only a few mouse-clicks behind 'music videos, general entertainment . . . or just people mucking around with a video camera.' YouTube, they suggest, provides a platform for exhibitionists, beyond the reach of Australian media regulators because of the international character of the

Internet. Young people are both agents and victims – responsible for the majority of YouTube's mundane content (teen-age hijinks and bedroom lip synching), much of its glorified hooliganism (car surfing, happy-slapping, public vandalism, and school-yard brawls), and at risk from exposure to footage of Hitler's speeches, racist propaganda, gruesome autopsies, dismemberment footage, and videos of mortar attacks in Baghdad.

This media panic convergence is exemplified by stories about 'cyberbullying' – the use of digital technologies to bully others, especially by posting humiliating or insulting videos, or by using video to document and celebrate acts of violence. In March 2007, the Victorian Government in Australia blocked access to YouTube from school property in part as a response to the uploading of a video showing twelve boys sexually abusing a 17-year-old Victorian girl (Smith, 2007). Similar calls to restrict access to the website to combat cyberbullying have come from teachers' groups and school boards in the UK ('Teachers in websites closure call,' 2007) and the US (Kranz, 2008). In response, YouTube launched its own anti-cyberbullying initiative – the Beatbullying channel ('YouTube tackles bullying online,' 2007).[2] The new category of cyberbullying, which academia has been complicit in creating (see, for example Patchin and Hinduja, 2006; Slonje and Smith, 2008), is a good illustration of how moral panics around youth, violence, and risk are linked to existing media effects discourses, producing a media panic (Drotner, 1999).

The media discourses around issues of morality in YouTube, the tone of alarm in Rawstorne and Crouch's 2,000-word demonization of the site, and the construction of the new category of 'cyberbullying,' can be seen as symptoms of uneasiness and uncertainty around media expertise and moral authority provoked by the mass uses of new media technologies such as mobile camera phones and the Internet for self-publishing. These moral panics are further amplified by the utopian hyperbole about 'Web 2.0' and the democratization of cultural production, because they can simply invert the value judgments without disturbing the assumptions underlying the trope of a user-led 'revolution.' It is the same myth of mass democratization as a direct effect of technological change that underpins both *TIME Magazine*'s announcement the 'Person of the Year' for 2006 was 'You' (Grossman, 2006b) and Andrew Keen's (2007) *The Cult of the Amateur*, which launched a polemical assault on participatory online culture on the grounds that it is eroding intellectual expertise and moral standards (35–46). In both cases, digital technologies are treated as if they directly cause the cultural transformations being celebrated or deplored.

The themes of these contemporary panics about participatory Internet culture are not as new as they appear to be. They mirror those that have occurred around the mass popularization of new media technologies and forms since early modernity. Concerns emerged around the pauper press in the early nineteenth century (Hartley, 2008b) and the emergence of the portable hand camera at the beginning of the twentieth (Mensel, 1991; Seiberling and Bloore, 1986), reproducing similar anxieties about the tools of cultural production or cultural record being in the hands of the masses – or more specifically, the 'children of the lower classes' (Springhall, 1999). Further, the mobilization of moral panic discourses is in some ways business-as-usual for the media these days when dealing with topics like new media, youth, and violence (see McRobbie and Thornton, 2002) – the discourse of the moral panic is now simply part of the professional repertoire of journalists. But, as Driscoll and Gregg (2008) note, one important point of difference in contemporary moral panics, particularly about the Internet, is that the 'establishment' discourses, as represented by the mainstream media, are less hegemonic than they were in earlier periods, and therefore less able really to contain the debates. Rather, they necessarily incorporate a wide range of dissenting views precisely because the web makes it possible to publicize a range of opinions.

Most importantly, the uses of YouTube that are the subjects of these media panics are not representative of the practices of the YouTube community as a whole. The offending videos uncovered by journalists often have received comparatively few views before their exposure in the national or international press, exposure that draws further attention to the very phenomena we are being encouraged to worry about. Based on the long history of this pattern of media panics, it is important we consider the extent to which moral panic discourses in public debates might actually amplify more risky, careless, or hurtful practices, while at the same time doing nothing whatsoever to exert a positive influence on the social norms that operate within the social networks that use YouTube as a platform.

Debates around good or bad uses of YouTube come down to ideas about ethics. But the ethics of participation in YouTube should not be reduced to making judgments about whether or not pre-determined moral standards are being lived up to. More pragmatically, ethics can be defined as the freedom and capacity to act reflexively – that is, to think about the ethical implications of one's own practice, and to formulate one's actions based on this ethical awareness, relative to a particular context. In the context of YouTube, ethical norms can be understood as the rules for practice that are continually being co-created, contested and negotiated in YouTube's social network. Given the long, repetitive history of interpreting new media as an articulation of risk, (im)morality, and youth, we might more productively seek to understand the extent and circumstances within which participation in sites such as YouTube involves reflection, ethical awareness, and care, as part of broader discussions about new media literacy, rather than as part of regimes of top-down control. Chapter 5 addresses this, describing how the user community engages actively in negotiating and contesting the social norms of participation on YouTube.

The Meanings of Amateur Video

A common assumption underlying the most celebratory accounts of the democratization of cultural production (Grossman, 2006a, 2006b) is that raw talent combined with digital distribution can convert directly to legitimate success and media fame. This assumption is especially noticeable in the mainstream media discourse around amateur video, usually invoking individual success stories that appear to realize this promise. For example, early in YouTube's history, the media interest in 'Lazy Sunday' turned the mainstream media spotlight on comedian Andy Samberg, at the time a new cast-member of *Saturday Night Live*. Samberg, along with writing partners Jorma Taccone and Akiva Schnaffer, came to the attention of the entertainment industry after posting their sketch comedy to the video-sharing website Channel101. com, which runs a monthly user-created film content, and on their own website The Lonely Island (Stein, 2006).[3] The success of their videos on these sites, especially *The'Bu* (short for 'Malibu'), their parody of US teen drama *The O.C.*, brought the team to the notice of Fox executives, who commissioned a pilot for a sketch comedy series (titled *Awesometown*). Though this series was not picked up, it did score the team a job writing for MTV, eventually landing them both in front of and behind the *Saturday Night Live* cameras. In another success story, home-made music videos featuring US band *OK Go* dancing on treadmills and in their backyard pushed the band into the mainstream after fans took the videos from the band's official website and uploaded them to YouTube (Adegoke, 2006a). Similarly, musician Terra Naomi secured a recording contract after becoming one of the most subscribed artists on YouTube musician's channel (Adegoke 2006a; Hutchinson, 2007). As recording labels and talent scouts increasingly turn their attention to online publishing opportunities (Bruno, 2007), YouTube has been mythologized as literally a way to 'broadcast yourself' into fame and fortune.

Cultural studies has a different view of how DIY celebrity works. Nick Couldry (2003) argues that in the mainstream media, the distance between 'ordinary' citizen and celebrity can only be bridged when the ordinary person gains access to the modes of representation of the mass media, making the transition from what Couldry calls 'ordinary worlds' to what he refers to as 'media worlds.' For Couldry, rather than blurring distinctions between the ordinary person and the celebrity, rags-to-riches stories and Reality TV alike *reproduce* the distinctions between the 'media world' and the 'ordinary world,' which 'disguises (and therefore helps naturalize) the inequality of symbolic power which media institutions represent' (2000: 16). The promise that talented but undiscovered YouTubers can make the leap from their 'ordinary worlds' to the bona fide 'media world' is firmly embedded in YouTube itself, evident in a number of YouTube's talent discovery competitions and initiatives. In response to the success of OK Go, YouTube created a dedicated channel for musicians to which 120,000 signed up in the three months between June 2006 (when the service was launched) and August 2006 (Adegoke, 2006a). Recent competitions for quality DIY content include the 'My Grammy Moment' competition, where YouTube musicians performed versions of the Foo Fighters' song 'The Pretender' on their chosen instruments in a bid to win a spot performing live with the band at the awards ceremony;[4] various short film competitions, including YouTube's first 'International Film Competition' in November 2007; the 'From Here to Awesome' contest in February 2008;[5] and the 'sketchies' comedy awards.[6]

Despite appearances, these examples do not in themselves realize the myth of DIY celebrity so much as they demonstrate its limits. In Graeme Turner's (2004; 2006) discussion of the topic,[7] he argues that the increased representation of ordinary people as potential or temporary celebrities in the mass media represents the 'demoticization' rather than the 'democratization' of the media. Even when ordinary people become celebrities through their own creative efforts, there is no necessary transfer of media power: they remain within the *system* of celebrity native to, and controlled by, the mass media. According to Turner, the 'demotic turn' in media culture relies on the existing structures of celebrity to deliver 'ordinary celebrity' which, far from providing alternatives to the existing media industry, is produced and captured by it.

Celebrity, at least as viewed through this frame, is not so different in YouTube. More accessible new media technologies and platforms can open up possibilities for the commercialization of amateur content, and in some cases turn the producers of that content into celebrities. But, as the examples discussed above show, the marker of success for these new forms, paradoxically, is measured not only by their online popularity but by their subsequent ability to pass through the gate-keeping mechanisms of old media – the recording contract, the film festival, the television pilot, the advertising deal.

Despite the prominence given to talent discovery initiatives in the mainstream media, YouTube press releases, and on the official YouTube blog, it is not self-evident that these initiatives have as much impact *on* the YouTube 'economy of attention' (Lanham, 2006) as they do on the mainstream media's conversations *about* YouTube. While much of the most popular content on YouTube comes from a variety of sources including mainstream media, YouTube has its own, internal system of celebrity based on and reflecting values that don't necessarily match up neatly with those of the 'dominant' media. There are YouTube celebrities who are famous for being notorious, obnoxious, or annoying: Chris Crocker of 'Leave Britney Alone!' fame[8] would certainly be one. But however spectacularly bizarre his performances may seem, Crocker's ongoing status as a 'star' YouTuber can only be achieved by ongoing participation *in* YouTube. This is quite different from the short-term flare of attention a *Big Brother* contestant receives at the whim of a television producer, or indeed the kind of celebrity associated with one-off viral videos that give the creators of the videos (or their subjects) their fabled fifteen minutes of fame. Additionally, there are YouTube 'stars' who, despite their carefully cultivated 'homegrown' brand identities, seem to be making a living via advertising revenue, reaching large audiences with content produced within and for YouTube, often with their own external websites as well.[9] They are not celebrities, famous for being famous; rather they are *stars*. Some of them, in fact, are famous for doing something in particular very well, even if that 'something' is unlikely to accrue prestige in the traditional media or arts industries. But, as Graeme Turner (2006) argues, this doesn't necessarily make the 'star system' of YouTube any more *democratic* than it is anywhere else.

There is another important dimension to the ways the DIY myth is articulated to the celebrity one. The rise to Internet fame the producers or subjects of 'viral videos' experience is represented as being all the more remarkable given the mundane, tasteless, or talentless qualities of amateur video. In a segment on YouTube from the ABC (US) Network's *20/20*, journalist John Stossel covers the perceived cultural range of amateur video, affecting a somewhat typical tone of incredulity in his opening address to the audience:

> Do you like watching kids doing stupid and reckless things?
> Animals doing cute things?
> Beauty queens falling down?
> Or a thousand prisoners dancing to the music of Thriller?
> It's all on YouTube.

It is possible to employ an alternative perspective here. Rather than amateur video being explained via the notion of the 'video about nothing' or by notoriety without talent, it could also be situated in the much longer history of vernacular creativity – the wide range of everyday creative practices (from scrapbooking to family photography to the storytelling that forms part of casual chat) practiced outside the cultural value systems of either high culture or commercial creative practice (Burgess, 2007). Amateur video on YouTube has just as much to do with the social history of the home movie – used to document the lives of ordinary citizens (Zimmerman, 1995) – as it has to do with exhibitionist consumers appearing on talk shows or being made over on 'ordinary television' (Bonner, 2003), and now racing to broadcast themselves. More broadly, interpersonal, playful, and identity-forming uses of information communication technologies (ICTs) have a long and well-documented history – exemplified in the famous example of rural women using telephones for group chat, going against the grain of the top-down intended uses of the technology for directly purposeful, business-like communication (Fischer, 1992). Learning from this history, as well as from observations of YouTube, it is important not to fall into the trap of simply assuming that vernacular video is organized

primarily around a desire to broadcast the self. Viewed as a form
of 'vernacular creativity,' the creation and sharing of videos functions culturally as a means of social networking as opposed to as
a mode of cultural 'production.'

One of the early hits of YouTube, the 'Hey Clip,'[10] illustrates
both the mainstream media perspective on amateur video – the
articulation of youth, gender, and DIY celebrity – and the vernacular creativity perspective, where formerly private media
consumption and cultural production are now a legitimate part
of the cultural public sphere. In the video, Lital Mizel and her
friend Adi Frimerman lip-sync, dance, play air guitar, and generally goof around to The Pixies song 'Hey.' The video was clearly
shot in several takes, and has undergone extensive editing so
that each cut is precisely in time with the beat of the song. It had
had several million views by mid-2006, remains one of the most
popular videos on the website, and had received more than 21
million views by March 2008. Demonstrating a sophisticated
understanding of the rules of the vernacular genre she was drawing on – the bedroom dance video – as well as a self-deprecating
awareness of its status *as* a vernacular form, Mizel explained the
motivation and meaning behind the video:

> We just turned on the camera and danced funny . . . I keep asking
> people why do you like it, and they say, 'Because it's reality.' You
> see it's homemade, that we're so spontaneous and natural –
> dancing, having fun. It makes people remember when they were
> young and danced in front of the mirror. (Kornblu, 2006)

The 'Hey' clip, along with the thousands of others like it, is both an
example and a witty and self-aware celebration of the mediatized
'bedroom cultures' of young people, particularly girls. Productive
play, media consumption, and cultural performance have always
been part of the repertoire of these semi-private spaces of cultural
participation (McRobbie and Garber, 1976; Baker, 2004), but
increasingly they have become 'publicized' via webcams, social
networking site profiles, and YouTube itself. Public media production and performance adds new dimensions to these circuits

of 'privatized media use' (Bovill and Livingstone, 2001). Webcam cultures – also associated with the online cultures of women and girls – had a significant history before YouTube, and early academic research and critique noted the implications of webcam culture for surveillance, shifting it from a vertical to a horizontal or 'participatory' model (Knight, 2000). In contrast to the exploitative mode of participation in Reality TV (Andrejevic, 2003), these authors argued 'cam-girls' had greater control over the conditions of both production *and* consumption of their own representations, so that webcam cultures should be understood at least as much in terms of 'empowering exhibitionism' (Koskela, 2004) as voyeurism. But, as with the 'moral' dimensions of participatory culture discussed earlier in this chapter, tensions between 'expression' and 'exhibitionism,' performance and surveillance are actively negotiated by the participants themselves. YouTube's vernacular producers attempt to control the 'publicness' of their participation in various ways, albeit with varying degrees of awareness of the extent to which relatively 'private' contributions might be accessed in ways outside of their control (Lange, 2007b).

The case of Bree, better known as Lonelygirl15, provides a particularly rich example that draws together various ways of understanding the role of amateur video, and points to the new relations of cultural production that make it hard simply to apply assumptions about the meaning of the amateur, the vernacular, and the everyday in the context of YouTube. Between July and September 2006, mainstream US media outlets such as *The New York Times, The Los Angeles Times,* and *The San Francisco Chronicle* became particularly enamored with Bree, a YouTuber vlogging[11] under the username Lonelygirl15. Her apparently emotional post on 4 July 2006 discussing troubles with her parents getting in the way of a burgeoning relationship drew half a million views in forty-eight hours, a significant increase from the 50,000 to 100,000 views a week her previous videos received (Davis, 2006: 238). Lonelygirl's videos were impassioned – they described a fraught relationship with her religious parents and played out the quandaries and capriciousness of her relationship with friend and fellow vlogger Daniel. Lonelygirl's posts eventually developed a stable viewership of around 300,000 views each.

Media commentators, especially *New York Times* blogger Virginia Heffernan[12] took an interest in the rapid fame of Bree, as well as the high level of speculation building in YouTube's user community regarding the authenticity of her videos. Though they fit the vlogging mould – a talking head speaking straight-to-camera, and covered the domestic, personal politics considered characteristic of the form, some of them looked 'too slick.' They were a little too well edited, and as a series, revealed a series of events that unfolded a little too much like a narrative for a personal journal.

The YouTube community was especially curious about these videos. Users began openly to query the authenticity of the videos in comments on YouTube, in online discussion, and in replies to blog posts. The press joined the debate, some guardedly discussed Lonelygirl and acknowledged the debate about whether Bree was a real vlogger while at the same time using her videos as an example to explore the creative capacities of young people (Murphy, 2006). Others, however, jumped headlong into the debate about her legitimacy (Chonin, 2006), especially once the truth was revealed: that the LonelyGirl15 'vlog' was really a film-making experiment by independent producers Mesh Flinders and Miles Beckett (Fine, 2006; Gentile, 2006; Heffernan and Zeller, 2006).

The case of Lonelygirl15 both supports and subverts the mythologies around the significance of YouTube's amateur content. Skillfully appropriating the aesthetics and formal constraints of the vlog and its confessional style, the Lonelygirl videos publicized and legitimized vlogging as a genre of cultural production. Arguably, however, it was the embeddedness within YouTube's social network of each character in the LonelyGirl15 universe that marked the videos as authentic: characters in the series used their own YouTube profiles and videos to introduce themselves and carry the narrative, as well as forging connections across other social networking sites such as MySpace. Bree,

Daniel, and other characters were made real not only through the skills of writers and actors, but also through their apparent use of YouTube to create and negotiate social relationships with other participants in the social network. Similarly, the 'gotcha' energies generated by Lonelygirl15 – the discussion around the authenticity of the characters and the series and the investigative efforts of YouTube users – point to the centrality of these social networking functions.

LonelyGirl15 violated the ideology of authenticity associated with DIY culture, while at the same time being wholly consistent with the way YouTube actually works. Though the series continued after the ruse was revealed, expanding beyond the bedroom locations to adopt something more of a cinema verité style, LonelyGirl15 introduced new possibilities for experimenting with and expanding the uses of the vlog form within YouTube. The possibilities of inauthentic authenticity are now a part of the cultural repertoire of YouTube; subsequent vloggers – such as the apparently awkward but earnest high-school boy daxflame – have built identities around a similar ambiguity about their authenticity. Trying to figure out how much of a given YouTuber's act is real (notable in the discussion around daxflame), or how big their production team is (a topic of debate in discussion around user LisaNova), demonstrates reflexive knowledge about the construction of YouTube videos that is now part of the mode of participation within the site – indeed a kind of game is built around the race to do the detective work involved in busting or confirming the myth of authenticity in each new case.

It is this social network function that is most noticeably absent from most mainstream media accounts of amateur and everyday content creation: the idea that the motivation for this activity might have at least as much to do with social network formation or collective play as it does self-promotion. In most discussions of user-created content, self-promotion is assumed to be a principal motivation. Amateurs are represented as individualistic, self-expressive producers who are mainly interested in 'broadcasting themselves,' rather than engaging in textual productivity as a means to participation in social networks. As a result, the collective practice of user-led content creation is sidelined in favor of individualistic narratives of web celebrity and self-expression, rather than an understanding of how amateur video as a *whole* – as represented by the flourishing genre of the vlog which, by far, preceded and extends beyond LonelyGirl15 – contributes to the production of value in YouTube through its sheer ubiquity and everydayness.

The Copyright Wars

The area where YouTube and the mainstream media actively interact most is, perhaps unsurprisingly, around questions regarding the website's status as a new platform for media distribution and consumption. Some incumbent media companies seem solely concerned with YouTube as a distribution system and, as such, debates about the site have been dominated by questions regarding the relationship between YouTube, Inc. and existing media companies, the advertising revenues that flow from the website, and the perceived copyright infringement of YouTube users. These debates are conducted on terms that struggle to engage with the issues regarding user rights and acceptable modes of participation in participatory culture that they raise.

Particularly in the lead-up to Google's acquisition, discussion on the technology and business pages pointed to the presence of copyright infringing content on YouTube as a possible encumbrance to sale or the expansion of YouTube's content offerings (Bawden and Sabbagh, 2006; Elias, 2006; Goo, 2006; Harris, 2006; Kopytoff, 2006; McKenna, 2006). Questions of infringement and the presence of copyrighted content contribute to a public perception of YouTube as primarily a distribution platform for the sharing of illegally reproduced proprietary content, particularly content made for broadcast. This perception of YouTube intersects with its constructions as a dangerous space – copyright infringement sets up a discourse about the threat to the entertainment industries posed by empowered but unchecked consumers.

Reporting about copyright is often responsive to events that fit with hard news values; we see stories about the saber-rattling by big business and large rights holders threatening lawsuits, and concerned about YouTube as a sanctuary for, or business built upon, copyright infringement (Blakely, 2007; Elfman, 2006; Karnitschnig and Delaney, 2006; Martinson, 2006). Reporting concerned with 'hard' technological innovation as YouTube develops and introduces (or fails to introduce) various Digital Rights Management strategies and other copyright controls makes up a second group (Geist, 2006; Letzing, 2007; Swartz, 2007; Veiga, 2006). Finally, we see stories about YouTube's copyright management strategies, the lawsuits actually leveled, the deals done, and the videos removed, reported because they are connected to the always-looming avalanche of lawsuits that might, at any moment, bring the company to its knees (Arthur, 2006; Charney, 2007; Li, 2006; Noguchi and Goo, 2006).

Discussion of these copyright wranglings has constructed a sometimes inaccurate narrative about the slow decline of broadcast media. YouTube's business model puts it in the 'reach' business, much like traditional media such as radio, television, and newspapers. The company has made partnership deals with content producers and offers revenue sharing deals with some of its most popular content providers. The service has also, at various times, been in talks with major American media players such as CBS, NBC, and Viacom about signing on as premium content providers (Delaney and Karnitschnig, 2007). But embedded within this narrative about YouTube as a savior of big media is a note of unease. The portrait is one of declining powers struggling to adjust to new modes of business and new structures of control, fueled by apocryphal tales of internally conflicted entertainment conglomerates whose marketing divisions upload content to the service only to have unaware legal departments request to have the same content removed (see Morrissey, 2006; Ryan, 2006; Wallenstein, 2006b).

As the success of 'Lazy Sunday' brought the service to public attention and the potential of the platform as a way to launch viral successes became accepted, large media companies including both NBC and Viacom began a cautious embrace of the service as a promotional platform (*PC Magazine*, 2006).[13] In March of 2006, after the removal of the 'Lazy Sunday' video proved YouTube to be 'trustworthy partners' in the eyes of NBC Universal's Chief Executive Jeff Zucker (Ryan, 2006), NBC was attempting to straighten out a deal to deliver clips of NBC content via the service. By 23 October 2007, however, talks had soured and NBC had moved all its content to 'private' status as it launched testing of its own premium content website Hulu.[14] Offering television programing and some films from the NBC Universal and Fox stables, media hype circulating around Hulu positioned it as a direct competitor to YouTube, delivering content and allowing users to embed clips from the service into their own webpages.

Positioning Hulu as a competitor to YouTube, however, once again bears out the mainstream media vision of YouTube as a distribution and promotional platform. While offering the ability to embed clips is a significant step forward for a mass-media-run website, and that functionality is one of the factors contributing to YouTube's early success, Hulu's focus on delivering content, rather than positioning audiences and content producers as participants in a social network, means the service provides none of the civic opportunity of YouTube that responds to many of the ways media consumers use content in their everyday practice. It is, instead, an online television delivery system.

Not long after the removal of 'Lazy Sunday,' US media conglomerate Viacom filed a lawsuit against YouTube and Google claiming $1 billion for copyright infringement (Hilderbrand, 2007). This followed a demand in late 2006 that the service remove upwards of 100,000 clips of Viacom content, including videos from Viacom brands Comedy Central, Nickelodeon, and MTV (Becker, 2007). Despite initially embracing YouTube – particularly for youth culture oriented channel MTV2 (Wallenstein, 2006b; Morrissey, 2006) – Viacom was less convinced by the end of 2006 of the promotional value of having videos on the service. Claiming programs such as Comedy Central's *The Daily Show* were among the most viewed videos on the website, and unhappy with the revenue-sharing deal they could negotiate, Viacom accused YouTube of unduly profiting from their labor.[15] 'YouTube and Google retain all of the revenue generated from [users uploading videos],' the company claimed, 'without extending fair compensation to the people who have expended all of the effort and cost to create it' (Karnitschnig, 2007). As YouTube sells advertising on some videos across the site, and doesn't police closely enough for Viacom's liking the uploading of copyrighted content without permission from copyright owners, Viacom argued YouTube not only profits from but has legitimated the uploading of content that infringes upon the copyrights of Viacom and others.[16] As the media conglomerate wrote in a press release shortly after filing their original motion:

> There is no question that YouTube and Google are continuing to take the fruit of our efforts without permission and destroying enormous value in the process. This is value that rightfully belongs to the writers, directors and talent who create it and companies like Viacom that have invested to make possible this innovation and creativity.[17]

Viacom were not alone; in mid-2008 Silvio Berlusconi's Mediaset took action against YouTube for 500 million Euros (US$780 million) for copyright infringement, TF1, the largest French broadcaster, filed suit for 100 million euros, ('UPDATE 2-Mediaset sues Google, YouTube; seeks $780 mln'), and the English Premier League announced action against YouTube for copyright infringement in 2007 ('Premier League to take action against YouTube').

There are questions that need to be asked about whether YouTube and Google really are profiting on the back of material produced by large media producers, especially as the arguments made by Viacom and others seem so soundly rooted in broadcast-era understandings of what media is and how it operates. There are questions about how we understand what is popular across the website, about how we understand what types of content it supports, and about the rights of both producers and audiences in a post-broadcast era.

While perhaps well within their legal rights, Viacom's actions conveyed a certain degree of disrespect toward the audience for their own programs. Online distribution – both through direct peer-to-peer technologies and online video sharing – is held to be partly responsible for the success of both *The Daily Show* and *The Colbert Report* (Goetz, 2005; Broersma, 2007). In fact, star of *The Colbert Report*, Stephen Colbert had made extensive use of YouTube up until that point, encouraging fans to post remixed videos of himself to the website. Colbert also gained both notice and notoriety when the US non-profit station C-SPAN demanded that a very popular clip of his performance at the 2006 White House Correspondents Dinner be removed, despite the fact that it was already freely available through the (then separate) Google Video service (Delaney, 2006). Beyond this incident, Viacom was at times clearly over-zealous in patrolling YouTube, resulting in both legitimate parodies and completely unrelated videos being claimed by accident (Mills, 2007).

The assertion that the videos that are 'Most Viewed' on the service constitute the *most popular* content treats YouTube as if it is just a distribution platform. As much as the site supports broadcasting-like activities, for some users the site is as much about discussion, response, and interaction with audiences and friends as it is achieving economies of scale for wide-spread distribution (Lange, 2007a). While Viacom's principal interest is finding the proportion of the overall archive composed of content they claim infringes copyrights, as we discuss in the following chapter, popularity on the service revolves as much around what is 'Most Discussed' or 'Most Responded' as it does what is 'Most Viewed.'

Understanding this is crucial to accounting effectively for YouTube as a diverse media space and to come to terms with the fact that YouTube is built as much through audience practices as it is through practices of publishing. As much as the video blog, YouTube is ruled by the clip and the quote – the short grab or edited selection that constitute traces of active audience-hood. Selecting and editing a particular moment might be seen as acts of what Fiske (1992b: 37–8) described as 'enunciative productivity,' creating and circulating certain meanings about objects of fandom. To see these only as acts of publishing or distribution is to impose broadcast-era understandings of how the media operates onto a service at the forefront of defining post-broadcast media logics. Copyright infringement and piracy are broadcast-era ways to deal with what are essentially audience practices. Indeed, as we suggest in the chapter that follows, that as audience practices, posting clips or quotes to YouTube more closely resembles what John Hartley (2008a: 112) describes as 'redaction' – 'the production of new material by the process of editing existing content,' (p. 112), than it does an act of copyright infringement or 'piracy.'

What the copyright wars illustrate particularly well is the difficult dual identity that YouTube, Inc. maintains. YouTube needs to be understood as both a business – where the arguments of Viacom *et al.* might be legitimate – and as a cultural resource co-created by its users – where these arguments strain for credibility. The truth is that both of these very different ideas of what YouTube is for are real and co-existing, if not always happily; at various times, as with disputes over claims of copyright infringement, the faultlines emerge.

YouTube as Mainstream Media

Amanda Lotz's book *The Television Will be Revolutionized* (2007) is one of the very first published scholarly works to deal with YouTube specifically. Her discussions of YouTube are evidently something of a late addition to the book, which was completed in late 2006, when it was only just beginning to receive a great deal of attention in the press and academia. On the implications of the proliferation of amateur video for industry production, cutting into demand, Lotz writes:

> By late 2006, it remained unclear whether the flurry of amateur video was merely a passing trend or likely to revolutionize television [. . .] Like so much of the new technological space, existing amateur video was largely confined to the efforts of high-school and college-aged students by the end of 2006. But as cultural

> discussion of YouTube grew, politicians and corporations quickly began adding their videos, creating an odd amalgamation spanning talking-head video of Ted Kennedy, Paris Hilton's music video debut, and cats using human toilets. (Lotz, 2007: 252)

We see here, in the absence at the time of scholarly work on YouTube as a cultural system, the use of a list of oddities to signify the diversity of YouTube. We also see the speed at which YouTube has continued to grow and the way that, even in the space of twelve months, it had become normalized as part of the mediascape. This is a pattern also borne out by the evolution of mainstream media discourse around YouTube – from oddity to the center of serious industrial, legal, and moral issues.

While mainstream media coverage continues to be characterized by a high degree of ambivalence about just what YouTube is and what it is for, there are increasingly indications that it is gradually becoming incorporated as a mainstream part of the cultural public sphere. The mainstream media deal with this as they have done before, by filtering the uses and meanings of YouTube through their own news values as well as through an ideological approach to emerging and popular media that refuses to admit that the vernacular uses of YouTube might have their own forms of legitimacy. Instead, they only admit YouTube's cultural significance when it can be shown to be articulated to traditionally legitimate forms of communication: mainstream political debate, as in the coverage of the YouTube/CNN debate as part of the lead-up to the 2008 US Presidential campaign (Feldman, 2007; Dilanian, 2007); or institutionally legitimized education and learning, as when various prestigious universities began uploading videos of entire lectures to YouTube (Alexander, 2007; E. Lee, 2007; Kessler, 2007).

YouTube has now arguably achieved mainstream media status; but just what kind of a medium is it? In YouTube, new business models and more accessible tools of production are provoking new and uncertain articulations between alternative media and the mainstream, commercial media; and throwing up anxieties about issues of media authority and control. These uncertainties could partly explain the oscillation between two dominant explanatory frameworks for the website – YouTube as a player in the commercial new media landscape on the one hand (the top-down view), and YouTube as a site of vernacular creativity and lawless disruption on the other (the bottom-up view). YouTube is not just another media company, and it is not just a platform for user-created content. It is more helpful to understand YouTube (the company and the website infrastructure it provides) as occupying an institutional function – operating as a coordinating mechanism between individual and collective creativity and meaning production; and as a mediator between various competing industry-oriented discourses and ideologies and various audience- or user-oriented ones. Without this audience-centered perspective, without a sense of how people use media in their everyday lives, any discussion of YouTube's cultural or social impact is likely to be based on a series of fundamental misunderstandings.

CHAPTER THREE

YouTube's Popular Culture

Accounting for Popularity

In this chapter we draw on a survey of some of YouTube's most popular content to establish some baseline knowledge about the range of uses people are making of the site. Understanding what YouTube might be for, and moving beyond moral panics about young people, the destruction of existing media business, copyright infringement, or the trivialities of user-created content, requires contextualizing YouTube's content with everyday media practices. Simply looking at content on YouTube doesn't give us the whole picture, of course – YouTube videos circulate and are made sense of on other websites; they are embedded in blogs, discussed in living rooms, and they are produced in rich everyday or professional contexts. But combining this knowledge with an analysis of the way particular *types* of videos move through YouTube as a system allows us to identify some of the most significant and interesting patterns in YouTube's popular culture.

This content survey draws on a sample of videos from four of YouTube's categories of popularity – Most Viewed, Most Favorited, Most Responded, Most Discussed. Across these categories, 4,320 videos were gathered by sampling from six days across two weeks in each of three months of 2007 (August, October, and November).[1] A coding system was developed to categorize these videos according to textual and extra-textual features, coding for origin, uploader, genre, and themes.[2]

This coding scheme involved two primary categories: the apparent industrial origin of the video (whether it was user-created or the product of a traditional media company), and the apparent identity of the uploader (whether a traditional media company, a small-to-medium enterprise or independent producer, a government organization, cultural institution, or the like, or an amateur user).[3] Our concern with the appearance of these videos, where they appear to come from and what they appear to be, is motivated by a desire to understand how content might be perceived and function within YouTube's ecology; by focusing on the apparent nature of the content coded, the study does not discriminate, for example, between 'pure' user-created efforts and supposedly user-created videos produced for viral marketing purposes or those seized upon by marketing campaigns. In practice, these are often indistinguishable, and to some participants, the role they perform is the same.

Our survey concentrated on the most popular videos within the time period of the study, partly because it helped to order our sample, but also because we were trying to understand some of the dominant patterns in popular uses of YouTube. Working through these patterns, in this chapter we attempt to locate the 'YouTube-ness' of YouTube – its shared and particular common culture – while respecting its complexity and diversity. We look not only at the mix of content that moves through the service but at the particular patterns of relations between videos on the website and the organization of YouTube itself.

But understanding how popularity works on YouTube requires more than simply identifying and describing which of the videos have been watched the most. Is the 'popular' simply a matter of degree – how popular a particular cultural product is, measured by its reach or sales? Or is it a matter of kind – the cultural forms that are loved intensely, or that are 'of the people'? Even within YouTube itself, content is represented as being more or less popular according to a range of different measures, including:

> *most viewed, most responded, most discussed, top rated, most favorited, previously popular,* and *most active* [4]

And it offers a range of different time periods:

> *today, this week, this month, and all time*

We concentrated on four of these categories of popularity – Most Viewed, Most Favorited, Most Responded, Most Discussed – because we (correctly, as it turns out) hypothesized that comparing across them would give us a sense of the way different kinds of video content are made popular by audiences in different ways.

Each of these measures of popularity orders YouTube according to a different logic of audience engagement. While all of these measures rely on quantitative assessments – they all count things – the categories Most Responded, Most Discussed, and Most Favorited provide a way to access measures of attention other than those that have predominated in the broadcast era. Whereas Most Viewed most closely resembles the aggregate measures of attention utilized by mainstream media industries as a way of counting 'eyeballs in front of the screen,'[5] each of the other three measures provides some account of popularity based on activities that signal a degree of participation in the YouTube community – if nothing else, all of them require the user to have an account. The Most Favorited category aggregates the videos popular enough to be added to a user's profile, and Most Discussed aggregates the videos that generate the most comments, whereas Most Responded records the videos that viewers were most frequently prompted to post a video response to, either by filming their own material or linking to another video in the system. Because it compares types of popular video content across these measures of popularity, this content survey doesn't simply tell us what is 'on' YouTube. Each of these ways of identifying YouTube's popular culture ends up constituting a different version of what YouTube is, and what it is for.

Because we were looking at a sample of the most *popular* videos, the results of this content survey are not simply a reflection of the collective tastes of the YouTube audience as a whole. The picture of what YouTube is and how it is used that emerges from the study is also partly shaped by the way popularity is measured, and the way popular content is represented on the YouTube itself.

Of course, in some ways, the popularity metrics do just what we might think – they measure the relative popularity of individual videos over a given time period, according to various criteria. But this is not all they do. They are not representations of reality, but technologies of re-presentation. Because they communicate to the audience what counts as popular on YouTube, these metrics also take an active role in creating the reality of what is popular on YouTube: they are not only descriptive; they are also performative.

Michel Callon (1998) makes the argument that economic theories of markets 'format' real markets by making them calculable, and therefore affecting the choices of real actors who participate in those markets. This is not the same as saying that the 'discourses' of markets 'socially construct' our choices; rather, our models and understandings of markets function technologically, producing knowledge that can be used in practice, but only within the constraints of the ways this knowledge is structured and presented. Much more modestly, the various measures of videos' popularity within YouTube function similarly: to a certain extent they make calculable and measurable a simplified and atomized model of audience engagement – based on the raw frequencies of views, comments, response videos, and additions to users' favorites. In turn, these metrics shape the character of the most popular content; users can either deliberately attempt to produce content that will achieve mass attention according to the preset criteria, or they can ignore them altogether (and receive attention from dramatically smaller audiences). As with the mainstream media interpretations of what YouTube is for, this produces a feedback loop between the perceived uses of and value logics of YouTube; and its 'actual' uses and meanings.

The Two YouTubes

The constructions of YouTube discussed in the previous chapter somewhat simplistically represent videos on the website as coming either from inside established media practice[6] or outside of it.[7] In doing so, YouTube is imagined as a space where these two categories co-exist and collide, but do not really converge: where familiar forms of mass media content will be encountered alongside amateur oddities; where television, cinema, music videos, and advertising, appear next to bedroom, boardroom, or back-yard productions. This dichotomy between the 'user-created' and 'traditional media' content is of course problematic for understanding YouTube as a site of new convergences and mutations of these categories, and so employing it analytically (as we have done) is an oversimplifying move. Nevertheless, it provides a useful organizing framework within which to begin a large-scale content survey, and our baseline division of the content into the categories 'user-created' or 'traditional media' produced some interesting results:

Table 3.1 Content Type Overall					
Number of Videos	MOST FAVORITED	MOST VIEWED	MOST DISCUSSED	MOST RESPONDED	TOTAL
Traditional	511	717	276	308	1812
User-Created	466	277	751	683	2177
Uncertain	103	86	53	89	331
Totals	1080	1080	1080	1080	4320

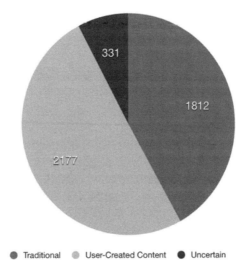

Figure 3.1. Content Type Overall

True to the 'Broadcast Yourself' promise of YouTube, the survey of the most popular content looks to be weighted, just slightly, in favor of user-created videos. Just over half the material, or 2,177 videos, were coded as coming from user-created sources – content produced outside of the mainstream, broadcast, or established media. A majority of these videos were vlogs (nearly 40 percent), the conversational form that is somewhat emblematic of YouTube's user-created content. Other genres included user-created music videos (15 percent) – including fanvids, and anime music videos;[8] live material (13 percent) – musical performances, sporting footage, and 'slice of life' footage; and informational content (10 percent) such as newscasts, video-game reviews, and interviews. Scripted material (8 percent) such as sketch comedy, animation, and machinima – animation made using video-game engines often created by capturing and editing choreographed gameplay – all made up a small part of the sample. New or unclassifiable genres, many of them exhibiting a fascination with the manipulation of technique rather than following any established form (discussed below) made up around 10 percent of the sample.

But contrary to the emphases of the mainstream media and some academic work on online video (see for example Aufderheide and Jaszi, 2008), there was a surprisingly small number of amateur, mundane, 'slice of life' videos in the sample – despite the myth, we just didn't come across very many cat videos at all. Nor were there *any* videos of children brutalizing each other, 'happy slapping' innocent victims, or 'hooning' around the neighborhood. This is not to deny the presence of this material on YouTube (clearly, it is there somewhere, along with knitting videos and vintage documentaries), but it did not appear in this sample of YouTube's most popular videos, which suggests to us its prevalence and popularity is generally overstated.

Almost 42 percent of the sample (1,812 videos) appeared to come from traditional media sources – videos originally produced within the established media industry, and frequently taken from an original source such as a television broadcast or a DVD, and then uploaded to the website without a substantial amount of editing. Popular genres here included informational programing (30 percent), which collected clips from major news services in the US, the UK, and Latin America, particularly material featuring 2008 US Presidential candidates, celebrity interviews, and appearances on talk shows, as well as portions from reality television programing. Scripted materials (21 percent) made up the next largest category, and included sketch comedy, animation, and segments from soap operas from Turkey and the Philippines. Videos from traditional media sources also included live content (17 percent) – predominantly sports footage, clips from US primary debates and music videos (13 percent), which came mostly from US Top40 artists. The final significant category included promotional materials (11 percent) – trailers for films and advertisements for products. Based on their titles and other studies of copyright content on YouTube,[9] it is probably the case that most of the videos that could not be coded because they had been removed came from traditional media sources.

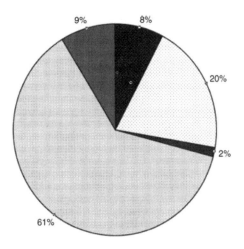

Figure 3.2. Uploader Types

Most of the videos seemed to have been uploaded by people outside established, mainstream media companies (see Figure 3.2). This group – coded as 'users' – was responsible for contributing a majority of the content in the sample – around 60 percent. Traditional media companies and large rights holders, a group that includes television networks such as NBC and organizations such as the NBA (National Basketball Association), who have traditionally patrolled their intellectual property rights fiercely on YouTube, made up only a fraction of the uploaders – about 8 percent. Between these two categories was a group described as 'Small-to-medium enterprises (SMEs) or Independent producers (indies),' those working within the professional media industry but outside the domains of big-media organizations. This group accounted for nearly 20 percent of the content uploaded.

When we compare user-created and traditional media across measures of popularity, some striking differences in how popular content is used begin to emerge (see Figure 3.3).

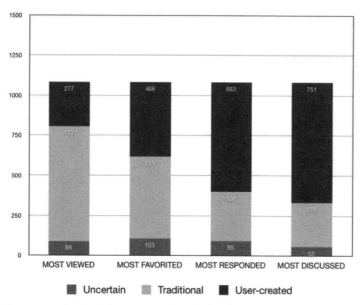

Figure 3.3. Content Types across Popularity Category

While user-created content dominates the sample overall, and 'users' appear to comprise the largest group of people contributing to the system, not all of the categories of popularity are dominated by user-created content. Though traditional media and large rights holders make up a small percentage of the overall uploaders – not surprising given the generally suspicious and cautious attitude taken by the majority of traditional media players we discussed in the previous chapter – content from broadcast and mass media sources comprises a significant proportion of the videos coded in the Most Viewed and Most Favorited (see Figure 3.3). Indeed, material from broadcast and mass media sources make up two-thirds (66 percent) of the Most Viewed category, where the largest genres were informational material – particularly news footage, political discussion, celebrity gossip, and interviews; live content – especially sports footage and live musical acts; and scripted programming – clips from television series, soap operas, and dramas, as well as animation and some sketch comedy. This content came mostly from television, but was mostly uploaded by users rather than by the traditional media and large rights holders themselves. User-created content in the Most Viewed category predominantly took the form of vlog entries, though there was also some instructional content, user-created sketch comedy, and musical performances – either footage from shows or users at home (or in the studio) performing directly for the camera.

The Most Favorited category – videos users have added to their personal profiles – was nearly evenly split between traditional (47 percent) and user-created content (43 percent). 'Favoriting' something is an act both of self-expression and identity perform-ance; when videos are added to a user's list of favorites, they're not just saved for later viewing; they are published as markers of personal taste and implicitly communicate recommendations to other users.

A portion of videos in each category of popularity was coded as 'uncertain'; these videos, comprising roughly 10 percent in the case of both Most Favorited and Most Viewed, included videos the coders were unable to make a definitive decision about. Many of the videos coded here had been removed from YouTube, and were undiscoverable on other video-sharing sites or elsewhere across the Internet. Others were from media systems coders were not familiar with – perhaps in a language other than English, Spanish, or Chinese – and coders were unable to read the formal, aesthetic, and extra-textual markers to determine the video's origin. Finally, some videos were coded as 'uncertain' in instances where coders could not clearly determine whether the content was user-created or the product of professional media producers, based on the content of the video and details provided in any intertextual or extra-textual sources, such as the profile of the uploader, hypertext links that might be provided to other sites on the Internet, or discussion in industry, press, or other publications regarding the videos.

These 'uncertain' videos reveal some of the most interesting difficulties that arise when classifying the content of YouTube. In practice, there is a great deal of slippage between the categories of 'traditional media' and 'user-created content' in our survey, and making determinations between them relies as much on how the material is positioned by extra-textual and intertextual material as it does on markers within the content itself. But these problems were also very productive: the coding process revealed some of the specific sources of uncertainty around the distinctions between professional and user-created content in YouTube.

Clips and Quotes: Uses of Traditional Media Content

Like all media, YouTube only really makes sense when understood as something that people make use of in everyday life. Bruns (2007) notes participatory culture and digital tools mean audiences no longer need to resort to auxiliary media forms to respond to the culture around them, suggesting the everyday experience of media audiencehood might need to be rethought to include new forms of cultural production that occur as part of ordinary media use. Participants in YouTube clearly do engage in new forms of 'publishing,' partly as a way to narrate and communicate their own cultural experiences, including their experiences as 'citizen-consumers,' which are bound up with commercial popular media. John Hartley (2008a) describes this mode of cultural meaning making as 'redaction' – 'the production of new material by the process of editing existing content.' For Hartley, redaction is:

> a form of production not reduction of text (which is why the more familiar term 'editing' is not quite adequate). Indeed, the current moment could be characterized as a redactional society, indicating a time when there is too much instantly available information for anyone to see the world whole, resulting in a society that is characterized by its editorial practices. (Hartley, 2008a: 112)

Hartley (2008a: 19–35) argues the origin of meaning has migrated along the 'value chain' of the cultural industries, from the 'author,' the 'producer,' and the text, to the 'citizen-consumer,' so that 'consumption' is a source of value creation, and not only its destination. Media consumption, under such a model, has moved away from being a 'read-only' activity to becoming a 'read–write' one.

This concept of redaction provides an alternative to the discourses of copyright infringement that dog the debates and corporate negotiations around the posting of traditional media content to YouTube. While some of the videos coded 'uncertain' discussed above have either been made private or removed by users,[10] the majority are unavailable as a result of copyright infringement claims by various parties, notably those identified as traditional media. A small portion is also unavailable apparently due to Terms of Use violations. This could signal a violation of YouTube's (very loosely defined) policies around offensive content, or (more likely) it may be the result of the user uploading copyrighted content – also a violation of the YouTube Terms of Use. Therefore the amount of material from traditional media sources is probably larger than our results suggest, given that during the delay between capturing and coding the data, a number of videos were removed due to copyright claims.[11]

There were several instances in this sample where the type of uploads media companies such as Viacom seem to dread most appeared – entire episodes of programming divided into sections. In particular, the sample included two soap opera series, one each from the Philippines and Turkey. Not only was this material flagged as copyright-infringing fairly quickly but, in both instances, the videos made for a poor-quality viewing experience. Although in early 2008 YouTube had begun to make announcements about the introduction of high-resolution video,[12] to date the low quality of YouTube videos,[13] and the ten-minute time limit imposed on uploads, have made it a poor technology by which to 'illegally' distribute copyrighted content,[14] especially compared to protocols such as BitTorrent, and compression technologies such as DivX and Xvid supported by some other video-sharing services. While YouTube's size makes it a significant site to explore the ramifications of digital distribution on the relationship between national boundaries and audience communities (Green, 2008), the uploading of traditional media content to the website is part of a more sophisticated range of cultural practices than simply the attempt to 'fileshare' or to avoid nationally or commercially bound distribution systems.

YouTube is filled with short 'quotes'[15] of content – snippets of material users share to draw attention to the most significant portion of a program. In terms of cultural analysis, the practice of quoting is quite distinct from that of uploading entire programs. Understanding YouTube as a redactional system, uploading is a meaning-making process, rather than an attempt to evade the constraints of mainstream media distribution mechanisms. Particularly through this practice of uploading media 'quotes,' YouTube functions as a central clearing house service that people use as a way to catch up on public media events, as well as to break new stories and raise awareness, as in the 'citizen journalism' model.

When video of campus police using a Taser on UCLA student Mostafa Tabatabainejad was posted to YouTube in November of 2006, the citizen jounalism potential of YouTube was elevated to the attention of the US national press. Frequently, however, quoted materials in the Most Viewed category, tend to reflect the topics already at the top of public agendas rather than breaking new stories. So we see, for instance, quite a number of highlights packages from qualifying matches for the 2008 UEFA European Football Championship, qualifying for which started in August 2007.

Unsurprisingly, the 2008 US Presidential election campaigning was well represented in the sample, in the form of campaign materials, debates, press clips, as well as commentary, discussion, and debate. This is to be expected given the increasingly significant role YouTube has played as a site for both top-down and grass-roots political campaigning (Jenkins, Forthcoming; Shah and Marchionini, 2007). The presence of such material could be taken as an indication of a significant degree of engagement in US politics by the YouTube community, and on popular rather than official terms. But arguably, the forms of political engagement hinted at in these videos have just as much to do with celebrity culture (Couldry and Markham, 2007) as they have to do with capital-P political culture – in the same way as the tabloid mainstream media focus on individual candidates as media personalities. Highlighting the effects on political life of the heightened and personalized media attention John Thompson (2005) calls the 'new visibility,' politicians' stances on issues and their positions on the political spectrum in some ways are nothing but backstory for the front-stage drama of their media appearances and 'gotcha' moments; and in the case of the minor Republican US presidential candidate Ron Paul, for a concerted attempt to drive up the popularity of an underdog candidate in defiance of the priorities set up by the mainstream media and the Democratic and Republican parties themselves.

In the light of our earlier discussions about the importance of understanding YouTube as part of everyday media use, it is especially significant that music videos were prominent in the Most Favorited category. Frith (1996: 110–11) argues music plays a central role for postmodern identity formation, its significance and

usefulness coming from its dual status as a marker of individu-
alism and a signifier of group participation. Music has likewise
been central to the formation of other social networking services (boyd, 2007) where it plays a significant role as a marker
of identity in user profiles, particularly of teens. The appearance
of music videos as a significant content type of Most Favorited
videos matches the identity forming function music plays, functions supported by social networking sites.

The patterns of cultural tastes and practices observed in our
study are undoubtedly related to those associated with the dominant forms of contemporary US popular culture more broadly
– characterized by an engagement with dominant media events
like the 2008 US Presidential Election; and by a preference for
humor, vernacular video, Top-40 music and teen idols, tabloid
culture, and celebrity gossip. But there is a certain 'YouTube-ness'
to these patterns as well. The intensity of engagement around
particular bands, artists, celebrities, and video genres is at least
partly produced within YouTube itself – how else to explain the
fact Ron Paul was, at times, more important to YouTube's attention economy than either Barack Obama or Hillary Clinton; or
the Jonas Brothers more adored than any other pop artist? The
patterns that emerged from the content survey hint at the shape
of YouTube's common culture – a 'structure of feeling' neither
unique to YouTube nor synonymous with web culture or popular
culture more broadly, however those categories are understood.

Vaudeville to Vlogs: User-Created Content

It is often assumed that YouTube is a platform built for amateur
creativity and that it thrives on user-created content. How much of
this content is represented as part of YouTube's popular culture?

User-created content makes up more than two-thirds of the
content coded in both the Most Responded and Most Discussed
categories, where it comprises 63 and 69 percent respectively – a
dramatically higher percentage than traditional media content,
especially when compared to the Most Viewed category, where

the situation was reversed.[16] As noted above, the sample included some but not large numbers of many of the prototypical user-created video forms. There were a few mundane videos, short films, fanvids, or hypercreative mashups, but there were also quite a few anime music videos, instructional video-game walk-throughs, as well as some examples of machinima.

Whatever the specific form, there were several observable aesthetic trends across the range of user-created content, indicative of the kinds of practices and values associated with an emerging medium. Frequently, the aesthetics of these user-created videos were especially concerned with experimentation with the video form, an explicit foregrounding of the medium itself that has historically been associated with the emergence of new media technologies, which Jenkins (2006c) suggests resembles the technological and aesthetic experimentation of vaudeville.

In many of the most popular user-created videos there was a noticeable focus on video as a technology, and on the showcasing of technique rather than of artistry. There was a large number of trick videos – using green screen technology, split screens, or reversed footage, as well as the use of techniques to foreground the technology itself, for example the use of sound processing to produce 'silly' comic voices. Two good examples of the creative combination of a trick concept with the capabilities of video recording and editing techniques are 'What Song is This?' in which the Star Spangled Banner is sung backwards live, and then the footage is reversed to reveal the song;[17] and 'The Original Human TETRIS Performance by Guillaume Reymond,'[18] a stop-motion animation in which a group of people dressed in various colors arrange and rearrange themselves in formation to imitate the progress of a game of Tetris, accompanied by an accurate *a cappella* version of the Tetris soundtrack.[19]

Another good illustration of this fascination with the technological capabilities of digital video editing is the category of videos referred to by their producers as 'YouTube Poop.'[20] Emerging as a genre of their own, these often-frenetic videos piece together found television footage into irreverent, often nonsensical works.

They show a particular fascination with Saturday morning cartoons from the 1990s (particularly 'low' American cartoons such as *The Super Mario Bros. Super Show!*) and television commercials, though there are also 'poops' made for anime series[21] and videos from YouTube itself.[22] The edits are often abrupt and jarring, and the audio is manipulated through quick cuts, changing speeds, and the introduction of alternative soundtracks. The result frequently foregoes narrative and resembles something most akin to parody or video art. Throughout the user-created content in our survey, regardless of the techniques used, the sample points clearly to a logic of cultural value centered for the most part around novelty and humor.

But it was vlog entries that dominated the sample, making up nearly 40 percent of the videos coded at Most Discussed and just over a quarter of the videos coded at Most Responded. The prevalence of vlog entries is significant given it is an almost exclusively user-created form of online video production. Vlogging itself is not necessarily new or unique to YouTube, but it is an emblematic form of YouTube participation. The form has antecedents in webcam culture, personal blogging, and the more widespread 'confessional culture' (Matthews, 2007) that characterizes television talkshows and reality television focused on the observation of everyday life. The success of Ze Frank (real name Hosea Jan Frank) was important in publicly defining the genre and establishing its possibility as a bona fide mode of cultural production, despite the fact it did not appear on YouTube. His 12-month vlogging project, 'the show with ze frank' which ran from 16 March 2006 to 16 March 2007, established some of the formal characteristics of the genre as it has been taken up in YouTube, particularly in terms of rapid editing and snappy performance to camera.

Jenkins (2006c; see also Butsch, 2000) notes vaudeville functioned as a relatively open platform for a wide range of short acts, each of which was kept under twenty minutes, and without directors, actors chose their own material and refined their skills based on direct audience feedback. There was a reliance on the emotional in order to create the memorable and the spectacular. Vlogging shares this emphasis on liveness, immediacy, and conversation and it is also important in understanding the particularity of YouTube.

The vlog reminds us of the residual character of interpersonal face-to-face communication and provides an important point of difference between online video and television. Not only is the vlog technically easy to produce, generally requiring little more than a webcam and basic editing skills, it is a form whose persistent direct address to the viewer inherently invites feedback. While television content – news, sketch comedy, clips from soap operas – may draw people to the service for a catch-up, traditional media content doesn't explicitly invite conversational and inter-creative (Spurgeon, 2008; Meikle, 2002) participation, as might be measured by the numbers of comments and video responses. It seems that, more than any other form in the sample, the vlog as a genre of communication invites critique, debate, and discussion. Direct response, through comment and via video, is central to this mode of engagement. Vlogs are frequently responses to other vlogs, carrying out discussion across YouTube[23] and directly addressing comments left on previous vlog entries. Patricia Lange (2007a) notes particularly engaged YouTubers directly address negative comments and 'hating' through their vlogs, many seeing this as an inherent part of the form itself. It is this conversational character that distinguishes the mode of engagement in the categories dominated by user-created content from those dominated by traditional media.

Two other significant genres in both Most Discussed and Most Responded were informational content and music videos. The former includes user-created newscasts, interviews, documentaries and a number of videos which would bleed over into the vlog category – they frequently critique popular media or comment on 'YouTube dramas' through visual juxtaposition, or by adding commentary or on-screen graphics. Many user-created music videos also adopt a conversational mode, as artists preface their work with a discussion of the motivations or context for the piece they have written or will perform, respond to suggestions and feedback, often drawing the audience into the intimacy afforded by direct address.

Some artists represented by large labels have taken up this mode as a way to engage and manage their fan communities. English/Portugese singer-songwriter Mia Rose is a good example of this. Rose represents herself as an independent artist, using YouTube to sell her content by reaching out across the social network to connect with her audiences.[24] In April 2008, after the sample had been captured, she signed to the NextSection Lifestyle Group and is now a managed artist with a major label. Her channel[25] remains unchanged, however, still projecting the same home-grown brand image with which it began. She remains, for all intents and purposes, an independent artist who is also a user of YouTube.[26]

Beyond the Professional and Amateur Divide

YouTube's popular videos are contributed by a range of professional, semi-professional, amateur, and pro-amateur participants, some of whom produce content that is an uncomfortable fit with the available categories of either 'traditional' media content or the vernacular forms generally associated with the concept of 'amateur' content. University lectures and educational materials, such as those uploaded by institutions including the University of New South Wales[27] and the University of California, Berkeley,[28] online presentations developed by Google for forthcoming products,[29] or footage of military aircraft landing uploaded by the Royal Australian Air Force[30] – each of these are examples of content which strain to fit anywhere in relation to the traditional media/user-created content dichotomy.

This dichotomy also fails accurately to characterize uploaders like Ford Models, who use YouTube for both promotional purposes and to identify talent.[31] Ford, much like Google, the RAAF, colleges and universities, is not a traditional media player; its presence on YouTube capitalizes on the same self-publishing and conversational opportunities as other non-media participants, despite their size. The material Ford produces – makeup tips, model profiles, fashion guidelines, and modelling tutorials[32] – could conceivably be packaged for broadcast as fashion programing on cable or broadcast television. Outside of the broadcast flow and contextualized within a branded YouTube channel, these videos appear as organic YouTube content; it is only the professional quality of the content and the corporate size of the uploader that would mark Ford Models as a traditional media player.

Similarly, the category of 'user' is complicated by web-tv start-ups, such as JumpTV Sports, who put together sports packages and deliver content to a range of sports sites around the world, and NoGoodTV, who produce vaguely risqué, masculinist, programming. Many of these uploaders resemble traditional television producers using the Internet as a way to distribute niche programming or specialized content without needing to negotiate cable or television distribution deals. NoGoodTV's content, for instance, resembles the laddish programming regularly seen on cable channels in the US such as Spike (a Viacom brand) and the video-game oriented G4 TV. It is a mixture of music videos, celebrity interviews, sketches, informational programing, and miscellanea, wrapped in on-screen graphics. Its resemblance to television content points to the way digital delivery options such as YouTube and the increasing move of material online are destabilizing medium-dependent definitions of media forms (Green, 2008).

So too, although videoblogging is a dominant form of user-created content and fundamental to YouTube's sense of community, not all vlogs are personal journal entries created in bedrooms. Indeed, a number of prominent vloggers, such as Nalts,[33] Charlestrippy,[34] and Blunty3000[35] are quite clearly using YouTube as a business venture. They participate in YouTube's advertising sharing scheme and draw revenue from their presence on YouTube. But unlike users like NoGoodTV who seem to bring to YouTube the same one-way model of participation we know from broadcasting, these producers are active participants in the YouTube community. Even though uploaders like Charlestrippy use their vlogs and YouTube pages to advertise their expertise – in his case, creating viral videos[36] – they are also active participants in the YouTube community. Their online success is as much due to their grounded knowledge of and effective participation within YouTube's communicative ecology as it is the savvy with which they produce content, and they are virtuosic in their mastery of YouTube's home-grown forms and practices.

To understand YouTube's popular culture, it is not helpful to draw sharp distinctions between professional and amateur production, or between commercial and community practices. These distinctions are based in industrial logics more at home in the context of the broadcast media rather than an understanding of how people use media in their everyday lives, or a knowledge of how YouTube actually works as a cultural system. It is more helpful to shift from thinking about media production, distribution, and consumption to thinking about YouTube in terms of a continuum of cultural participation.

This requires us to understand all those who upload, view, comment on, or create content for YouTube, whether they are businesses, organizations, or private individuals, as *participants*. For one thing, content is circulated and used in YouTube without much regard to its source – it is valued and engaged with in specific ways according to its genre and its uses within the website as well as its relevance to the everyday lives of other users, rather than according to whether or not it was uploaded by a Hollywood studio, a web TV company, or an amateur videoblogger. All contributors of content to YouTube are potential participants in a common space; one that supports a diverse range of uses and motivations, but that has a coherent cultural logic – what we refer to as the YouTube-ness of YouTube. Likewise, this model asks us to understand the activities of not only content creators but also audiences as practices of participation, because the practices of audiencehood – quoting, favoriting, commenting, responding, sharing, and viewing – all leave traces, and therefore they all have effects on the common culture of YouTube as it evolves. Those who insist on treating YouTube as if it is a broadcasting platform are probably less likely to achieve the aims of their participation, whatever they may be.

CHAPTER FOUR

YouTube's Social Network

So far we have discussed various modes of engagement and participation that occur within and around YouTube, including not only original content creation, but also the repurposing, annotation, and remixing of traditional media content. The previous chapter highlighted the importance of understanding that in YouTube, content creation is probably far less significant than the *uses* of that content within various social network settings. Video content from a wide range of sources is uploaded to YouTube for an equally wide range of communicative purposes, embedded in various existing or emerging taste communities, media subcultures, and fandoms.

Most people are far more likely to watch videos hosted on YouTube than they are to log into the website regularly, let alone to create and upload videos (Madden, 2007). But for a small proportion of users, YouTube is a social network site. Unlike the more obvious social network sites such as Facebook, where social networking is based on personal profiles and 'friending' (boyd and Ellison, 2007), in YouTube the video content itself is the main vehicle of communication and the main indicator of social clustering (Paolillo, 2008; Lange, 2007b). In this chapter, we understand the users who spend time on the website contributing content, referring to, building on and critiquing each other's videos, as well as collaborating (and arguing) with one another, as constituting YouTube's 'social core' (Paolillo); and in terms of innovation theory, a group of 'lead users' who collectively identify and exploit opportunities to improve the way YouTube works through their own practices (Von Hippel, 2005). We argue that the activities of these 'YouTubers' (a category that operates in the community itself as well as in academic discourse (as in Lange, 2007a) are very important drivers of the attention economy of YouTube, and significant in the co-creation of a particular version of YouTube's emergent culture.

The difference between the Most Subscribed and the Most Viewed 'channels' (the name given to the profile pages of particular contributors) of all time as at February 2008 illustrates this clearly.[1]

Table 4.1. Most Subscribed and Most Viewed Channels		
	Most Subscribed (all time)	**Most Viewed (all time)**
1	smosh	universal music group
2	universal music group	sonybmg
3	kevjumba	CBS
4	nighiga	SouljaBoy
5	HappySlip	mYcheMicalromaNce
6	esmeedenters	linkinparktv
7	miaarose	smosh
8	lonelygirl15	BritneyTV
9	WHATTHEBUCKSHOW	TNAwrestling
10	JamesNintendoNerd	esmeedenters
	Homegrown YouTube 'Stars'	Extension of Traditional Media Brand

As Table 4.1 demonstrates, while traditional media companies are well represented in the Most Viewed list, the list of Most Subscribed channels is dominated by 'YouTube stars' – participants (whether strictly 'amateurs,' SMEs, or even musicians backed by major labels) whose brands were developed within YouTube's social network. Their work covers a range of genres, from sketch comedy films (smosh) through celebrity news (WHATTHEBUCKSHOW), and comedy-style vlogging based around everyday life and personal identity (kevjumba, happyslip). In comparison to the Most Viewed category, the list of Most Subscribed videos contains far fewer traditional media companies like music labels (such as Universal Music Group) or sports franchises (TNAwrestling), using YouTube as a platform for brand extension.

These two categories sit at opposite ends of the spectrum of engagement on YouTube. The Most Viewed category, as for videos, simply measures the number of times a particular channel page has been viewed – representing the channels that may not draw an especially high level of intensity or direct visible engagement, but have the greatest reach. The Most Subscribed category contains those channels that the most users want to follow (or, perhaps, to publicly perform following). In aggregate it is a result of the actions of users who have a user account, and it represents a collective performance of what the YouTube community values most.

YouTube, Inc. as Patron

In her study of online photosharing and cellphone technologies, Virginia Nightingale (2007) draws on the anthropologist Alfred Gell (1998) to elaborate theories of agency and exchange as forms of participatory culture that take place at the nexus of corporate-controlled technological systems and everyday life. As Nightingale explains, Gell suggests patronage partly predetermines 'the conditions under which the creative work is produced and the environment of reception in which the image is displayed' (Nightingale, 2007: 293). In the context of camera phones and image-sharing websites, 'industry players maintain the ongoing operational environment and offer "patronage" to site users.' Likewise, YouTube, Inc. can be seen as the 'patron' of collective creativity, controlling at least some of the conditions under which creative content is produced, ordered, and re-presented for the interpretation of audiences. In previous chapters, we have described the ways in which, for example, the YouTube website's metrics of popularity order our understanding of what YouTube is for; as well as the impacts on aesthetics of YouTube's technical limits, such as the short video duration and the low resolution; and the shaping effect of the aesthetics of the user interface.

But the purposes and meanings of YouTube as a cultural system are also collectively co-created by users. Through their many activities – uploading, viewing, discussing, and collaborating – the YouTube community forms a network of creative practice. Writing about the social worlds of various fields of cultural production, from modernist poetry to dancehall jazz and avant-garde music, Howard Becker (1982) described this kind of formation as an 'art world' – 'the network of people whose cooperative activity, organized via their joint knowledge of conventional means of doing things, produces the kind of art works that art world is noted for' (Becker, 1982: x). Becker's case studies demonstrate the ways that aesthetic principles and technologies are shared by producers, support workers, and audiences, and the way they organize, enable, and constrain the possible range of a particular artistic activity. The construction and negotiation of aesthetic values and 'proper' techniques, he argues, is not confined to academics or experts, but involves everyone who contributes to the process of cultural production, including audiences. Similarly, in YouTube, aesthetic values, cultural forms, and creative techniques are normalized via the collective activities and judgments of the social network – forming an informal and emergent 'art world' specific to YouTube.

As patron, YouTube, Inc. provides the supporting and constraining mechanisms of a system whose meaning is generated by the uses to which the website is put, and within which, collectively, users exercise agency. The political implications of this arrangement, however, are undecided – with a recent proliferation of scholarship arguing that the participation of user communities can be read in terms of 'affective,' 'immaterial,' and even 'free' labor (Terranova, 2000). Critiques of the creative industries discourse point out the implications of this for the work conditions of creative practitioners and media professionals who are already under-compensated, and who work within conditions of 'precarious labor' (Deuze, 2007; Ross, 2000), pointing to a crisis of uncertainty in the economic structures of the cultural industries especially highlighted by the Writers' Guild of America strike in 2007. Others are concerned with the various ways platform providers such as game publishers profit directly from user productivity while simultaneously constraining users' rights (Humphreys, 2005a).

As in the case of Massively Multiplayer Online Games (MMOGs), YouTube, Inc.'s role is not that of a producer but that of a platform-provider: indeed, even more so than in games, its value, meanings and possibilities – what we mean in general conversation when we say 'YouTube' – are produced out of the collective work and play of its users. But the more literal versions of labor-based critiques may not be helpful in understanding the economic transformations that accompany these new models of user-participation in cultural production.

Drawing largely on ethnographic work with both MMOG players and game developers, Banks and Humphreys (2008, n.p.) argue these new relations of cultural production indicate a profound shift in which 'frameworks and categories of analysis (such as the traditional labor theory of value) that worked well in the context of an industrial media economy are perhaps less helpful than before.' They argue these relationships in fact 'introduce a form of creative destruction to labor relations' in contexts where all the participants (including 'producers' as well as 'user co-creators') have mixed motivations, and where they work for a range of benefits. Some gamers engage in co-creative activities out of a passion for the game itself, others for the pleasures of achievement, others for social status within the game community, and still others in pursuit of commercial opportunities. As Banks and Humphreys also note 'producers, programmers, artists, community development managers, and CEOs' have a wide range of often conflicting ideas about how the new collaborative and co-creative production processes of game environments should be managed, but that 'it is from these uneven, multiple and messy practices, motivations, nego-tiations, actants, and materials that participatory culture is being made and negotiated.'

YouTube is a relatively new site of the same kinds of 'messy' and emergent relations among platform providers, content pro-ducers, and the audiences Banks and Humphreys describe. In the rest of this chapter, we investigate the way these new models of cultural production and participation play out in YouTube and how they are understood and negotiated in practice by the 'YouTubers.' In the ordinary course of their cultural practice as YouTubers, these most visibly engaged users of YouTube actively participate in shaping, contesting, and negotiating the emergent culture of YouTube's social network, the idea of a YouTube community, and their relationships to the company's interests.

YouTubers as User Innovators

One of the more striking features of YouTubers' community-oriented activities is that they take place within an architecture that is not primarily designed for collaborative or collective par-ticipation. In comparison to other social networking sites built around user-created content, like Flickr and LiveJournal, and despite the rhetorical address to the YouTube 'community' in the company's official blog, the architecture of YouTube does not overtly invite community-building, collaboration, or purposeful group work. Harley and Fitzpatrick (2008, n.p.) note that the top-down conceit of YouTube as an alternative 'broadcaster' (rather than a social network) flows through to interaction design ele-ments that work to 'filter out' the social network aspects of the website for the casual or novice visitor or user. The website's visual design is consistently dominated by thumbnails of videos, not user profiles, groups, or conversations; groups are far from easy to find using keyword searches and, like videos, they are ranked quantitatively.[2] The ban on downloading and the absence of user-control over licensing creates serious barriers to collaborative production – there are no *overt* invitations to collaborate with other users, or to remix or quote each other's videos.

YouTube's interface design may not be elegant, but it is famously *usable*, at least within the limits of its assumed purpose – to upload, transcode, tag, and publish videos. Indeed, its usability is undoubtedly one of the reasons for its mass popularization. But this apparently seamless usability can also be seen another way – as both a constraint and an unstable compromise. Technologies designed for active user participation (like software, digital cameras, or YouTube itself) generally represent a compromise in design between two ideological extremes. At one end is the ideal of extreme *hackability* – 'where a given technology is perceived and presented as open-ended, manipulable, and affording complex experimentation with an accompanying level of difficulty' (Burgess, 2007: 89). At the other is the ideal of extreme *usability* – 'where a technology is perceived and presented as allowing easy access to a pre-determined set of simple operations' (Burgess, 2007: 89). As technologies stabilize and become widely adopted, compromises between the two are always reached. Ideally, the tensions between these competing dynamics are never really resolved, opening up possibilities for highly usable and accessible technologies that are also expansible, adaptable, and malleable (Galloway *et al.*, 2004), and so preserving the potential for the technologies to be 'generative' (Zittrain, 2008) of new or unexpected possibilities. Even the most usable and apparently simple technologies may offer creative possibilities that extend far beyond their most obvious, invited uses – possibilities most frequently realized (or even pioneered) by users, often to the surprise of the technology's designers.

Similarly, despite YouTube's design focus on usability and a simple and limited set of features, a number of interesting and innovative uses of YouTube have originated in the user community. For example, live video chat, which is a popular activity elsewhere, has not been introduced as a YouTube service to date because of perceived privacy risks (Stone, 2007). As a workaround, many of the most invested YouTubers are using relatively unregulated alternatives like Stickam,[3] the social network site based around live video chat, as a supplementary technology, maintaining consistent usernames across the two websites, and so effectively adding a 'plug-in' to YouTube. The use of Stickam amplifies the social network affordances of YouTube and allows the YouTubers to build their brands using ambient, 'always on' technology, rather than only through the production of static episodes of their vlogs.[4] Such a work around is necessary given the social networks that make use of YouTube are mobile and multiple, not contained within YouTube's architecture or technologies. The microblogging service 12seconds.tv, launched in mid-2008, similarly spawned a flurry of cross-registrations, resulting in a YouTube 'meme' built around 12-second vlog entries.

Despite its community rhetoric, YouTube's architecture and design invite individual participation, rather than collaborative activity; any opportunities for collaboration have to be specially created by the YouTube community itself, or by special invitation from the company. YouTube provides no built-in, routinized methods of capturing video from other users and reusing it, or of making one's own content available for this purpose. Nevertheless, collaborative and remixed vlog entries were a very noticeable feature of the most popular content in our survey. Sometimes, it was clear that a significant amount of planning had gone into the production of these videos and that they were attached to purposeful aims (like influencing the rankings, celebrating an event, and so on). At other times they appeared to function as ways of celebrating and representing YouTube as a community of practice. Within weeks of the launch of 12seconds. tv, several prominent YouTubers participated in a 12-second collaborative vlog entry posted at 12seconds.tv and linked to from a longer, individually produced vlog entry by fantasticblabbings. Fantasticblabbings used the cross-post to discuss the proliferation of online identities across social network sites, expressing scepticism with regard to the faddish adoption and abandonment of these sites.[5] This provides an illustration of the extent to which

YouTubers, as cultural agents, are not captive to YouTube's architecture, and demonstrates the permeability of YouTube as a system. It connects with surrounding social and cultural networks, and users embedded within these networks move their content and their identities back and forth between multiple sites. YouTube has never functioned as a closed system, from the beginning providing tools to embed content on other websites like blogs. Viewed in this light, it is surprising that this porting of content to and from the website is not more actively supported by the service itself.

There are a number of more subtle things users do to make up for perceived lacks or missing affordances in the provided technology. For example, even though the technologies needed to embed clickable links or user-contributed annotations and comments within video streams have existed for quite some time, up until mid-2008 no such capability had been introduced into YouTube, and the ability to refer back to other YouTube videos as part of each new utterance in a conversation was likewise very limited. Adrian Miles' (2006) experimental and theoretical work on networked video and hypertext cinema centers on these questions of video's potential to become more like blogging, to be 'porous to the network,' and 'to allow quotation, interlinking and to develop a media which is as permeable and granular as networked text' (Miles, 2006: 221). While this potential is very far from being realized, some of YouTube's competitors already offered the ability to tag and annotate other users' videos with comments, attached to various points in the video timeline.[6] When YouTube did eventually add annotation to videos, its use was limited to the owners of the videos (presumably to avoid an onslaught of annotation spam). So YouTubers developed their own solution to the problem, collectively instituting conventions to work around the absence of true media richness and interactivity – we observed several instances in which hyperlinks had been added as annotations in the texts of video descriptions or had been superimposed as graphics over the video footage, and then the performer physically pointed to the appropriate place on the screen to draw attention to the link. The collective development of analogue solutions like this to perceived technological limitations hints at the strong desires of the YouTube community to embed their video practice within networks of conversation, rather than merely to 'broadcast themselves'; and their willingness to find ways to do this even if not supported to do so by the provided technology.

User-led innovation in YouTube also extends beyond 'hacks' of the technology to include *content* innovation – creative adaptations of the existing conventions of online video. In particular, the very basic formal rules of the vlog entry – a talking head, a camera, some editing – are used as the basis for collective creativity and innovation. Some examples of innovations on the basic prototype of the vlog entry include the use of shot-reverse-shot-style editing to create the impression of the vlogger having a conversation with herself; the use of split screens and green screens; and a significant and growing level of generic hybridity, so that musical performances, stand-up comedy, and life-blogging merge and recombine to create new generic conventions and expressive possibilities.

The production and circulation of these vlog entries also provide an environment for reflexivity and activism within YouTube's social network. The results of our content survey revealed some patterns in the ways vloggers represent themselves as active participants – even activists – in the ongoing process of shaping and negotiating the meanings and uses of YouTube. As a starting point, we conservatively estimated that a substantial proportion – at least 10 percent – of the most popular YouTube videos uploaded between June and November 2007 were explicitly concerned with YouTube itself. Of these, more than 99 percent were user-created; that is, almost none of these videos that were in some way *about* YouTube were coded as traditional media content. This finding is obvious in retrospect, because the mainstream media do not, as a rule, make much content specifically for YouTube, even though they do produce content destined generally for the web. If they were to make content for YouTube, it is almost certain to be designed around their own brands, and not the YouTube brand or its audience.

The user-created 'meta YouTube' videos range widely in their forms and modes of address, from collaborative montages that evoke a sense of community to simple slideshows using text and music that invite responses in a bid for popularity. Tellingly, a full two-thirds of these videos were vlog entries. In general, vlog entries implicitly address an audience of fellow YouTubers along with a wider imagined audience. One of the basic communicative functions of the vlog entry is purely phatic – it announces the social presence of the vlogger and calls into being an audience of peers who share the knowledge and experience of YouTube as a social space. But these specifically YouTube-focused vlog entries do something else as well: making videos about some aspect of YouTube demonstrates, and in fact requires, a reflexive understanding of how YouTube actually operates as a social network, rather than as a distribution platform that can be used to broadcast to an online audience.

Vlogging tends to be canny and knowledgeable about YouTube's attention economy, with all its many faults, and this knowledge is often performed playfully or humorously, even when the video critiques some aspect of the way the website measures and rewards attention. The measures of popularity we discussed in the previous chapter are increasingly the target of gaming strategies on behalf of marketers – there are even companies that offer to send videos 'viral' for a fee. The YouTube user community is well aware of this – their discourse reveals a perceived link between the common characteristics of the most popular content (which seems to them to represent an inauthentic overvaluation of sex, shock and stupidity); and the actions that need to be taken by content creators in order to gather audiences.[7] Some videos cheerfully exploit this knowledge of the value system of YouTube's common culture; some actively critique it. Whatever the perspective, these videos indicate that the most active participants in YouTube are highly knowledgeable – perhaps even more so than the company itself – of the specific ways in which these measures of popularity can work to support or disturb what they see as the authentic, 'bottom-up' culture of YouTube.

This mode of communication – performing insider knowledge in an entertaining way while also making interventions into the culture of the YouTube community – is evident in OhCurt's video 'Mission Improbable: An Almost Shout-Out,'[8] which was one of the most discussed videos in our sample. The video is a collaborative vlog sketch in which OhCurt play-acts telephone conversations with the other YouTubers he is nominating in his response to yet another YouTuber's 'tell me 5 cool channels' invitation. The humor of the sketch is based around farcical miscommunications and misunderstandings between YouTube participants, and gently parodies the banality of the 'shout-out' tradition.

Shout-out invitations are one example among many of the ways in which the self-constituting YouTube community introduces tactics to attempt to navigate, shape and control the otherwise vast and chaotic array of content that exists in the network. These kinds of videos represent situated creativity (Potts *et al.*, 2008b) and reflexivity on the part of the YouTubers, constructing a YouTube that functions as a communicative space and a community (rather than an inert distribution platform for content produced in different contexts like television, for example). The YouTubers who participate in these ways are by definition 'lead users' (Von Hippel, 2005) – they are both early adopters of new technologies, ideas and practices, and significant agents in the development of innovations that better serve the needs of the user community. This does not necessarily mean that these lead users are exceptional individuals. Rather, user-led innovation of this kind appears to be simply a fundamental part of the way YouTube works; an effective lead user is one who understands the way the system works and can mobilize their own skills and capacities in ways that make sense within that system.

The conclusion to be drawn from these observations is that in order to operate effectively as a participant in the YouTube community, it is not possible simply to import learned conventions for creative practice, and the cultural competencies required to enact them, from elsewhere (e.g. from professional television production). 'Success' (measured by gaining large numbers of loyal subscribers, having videos 'featured' or receiving millions of views per video) appears to be gained by effectively exploiting these site-specific competencies. This requires some rethinking around what we might mean by digital literacy, and how the skills that count as literacies are acquired, shared, and learned, in the context of user-created content communities like YouTube.

Literacy and the Social Network

Digital literacy is one of the central problems of participatory culture. At least in the most technologized societies, earlier concerns around the unevenness of online participation focused around the idea of a 'digital divide' – a matter of access to technology – have given way to questions about digital inclusion and participation (Warschauer, 2003). The notion of the digital divide was a binary concept based simply on the access, or lack of access, to digital technologies like computers or broadband infrastructure. In such a construction either you were digital, or you weren't. Although access is still a huge issue, debates have shifted to encompass the idea of a 'participation gap' (Jenkins *et al.*, 2006): at its heart, a matter of literacy.

The long history of literacy, from print to media, brings with it a number of important debates relevant to the idea of a participatory culture. Sonia Livingstone (2004) proposes most discussions of new media literacy are characterized by historically unresolved tensions between 'critical' or 'Enlightenment' views of literacy – polarized philosophical positions that see literacy as a normative and exclusionary construction on the one hand (the 'critical' view); or as an aid to progress and equality we should aim to extend to all people on the other (the 'Enlightenment' view). Proving Livingstone's point, the US media literacy movement variously frames literacy as empowerment or therapy for the dangers of the media (or both; see Hobbs, 1998). The near-ubiquity of digital technologies means creative practice is necessary for both critical awareness and informed participation in the media. On the one hand, young people in particular might be learning new media competencies through their participation in YouTube (Drotner, 2008); and at the same time, according to the media literacy framework, this active and creative participation might also be used to help young people learn to be more 'critical' of media messages (Jenkins *et al.*, 2006). In the UK also, the definition used by the national media regulator Ofcom reflects this new emphasis on the interrelatedness of 'writing' as well as 'reading' competencies – it defines new media literacy as 'the ability to access, understand and create communications in a variety of contexts.'[9]

A second set of questions cluster around the problem of how to define, measure, and build capacity for literacy. The apparent proliferation of possible modes of communication using digital technologies has given rise to an equally wide range of qualifiers for the noun 'literacy' – visual literacy, media literacy, multimedia literacy, network literacy, and so on ad infinitum. Rather than giving in to the pressure 'to determine precisely and authoritatively which practices [. . .] legitimately fall under the rubric "literacy"' (Collins and Blot, 2003: 3), it is perhaps more important to acknowledge that the endless stream of 'kinds' of literacy indicates something about the current period of social instability around its relationship with media technologies. Indeed, Collins and Blot (2003: 3) suggest literacy has a status approaching that of 'science' in the nineteenth century: it 'refers loosely to any body of systematic useful knowledge.' This indeterminacy also hints at what is probably the most important point: 'literacy' is not a self-evident thing individuals can possess, and nor are any of the possible specific 'literacies.' Literacies, rather, are produced by, and practiced in, particular social and historical contexts.

Since at the current moment both media and knowledge are in a state of flux, so too is the definition of literacy. Our approach is closely aligned with New Literacy Studies movement (Street, 1984), where instead of literacy being a 'technology of the mind' or set of skills (i.e. an internalized competency or range of competencies that can be attributed to or possessed by an individual human agent) it is considered a social practice. The most important outcome of these debates should be to understand that new media literacy is not a property of individuals – something a given human agent either possesses or lacks – but a *system* that both enables and shapes participation. It still follows, however, that it is possible (and necessary) within this conceptual framework to talk about the individual competencies required to participate effectively in this system. The questions of how this system is shaped and who has access to it represent the key political questions of new media literacy.

Being 'literate' in the context of YouTube, then, means not only being able to create and consume video content, but also being able to comprehend the way YouTube works as a set of technologies and as a social network. For our purposes, what counts as 'literacy' is at least partly specific to the culture of YouTube itself. Individual competencies and knowledges are required, but not all of them can be imported from elsewhere. It is important to also note that, in our observations, while requiring a pre-existing familiarity with digital technologies and online culture, these competencies are not in-born natural attributes of the so-called digital natives (Prensky 2001a, 2001b). Indeed, many, if not most, of the most prominent 'lead users' – those whose videos gain the most attention and therefore those who are able to find an audience for their views or to mobilize other users – are adults in their twenties or thirties.

Peter Oakley, a British vlogger in his eighties known on YouTube as Geriatric1927, provides a good example of how YouTube-specific competencies can be learned and mobilized through participation in YouTube's social network. Oakley has been a consistently high-profile celebrity on YouTube since August 2006, when his first videoblog post – a brief and tentative experiment with a webcam and Windows Moviemaker humbly titled 'First Try,' exploded onto the Most Viewed page of YouTube's popularity rankings (largely because of the novelty, at the time, of his age).[10] That first video, as of March 2008, has received more than two-and-a-half million views, and Oakley remains a regular and very engaged member of the YouTube community, posting on topics such as the making content for YouTube and the ethics of online behavior and 'haters.' By tracing his contributions to the website over time, it is clear Oakley has used his YouTube presence to reflect on and develop his own creative and technological competencies – progressing from basic straight-to-camera vlogs using Windows Moviemaker to the integration of photos with overlaid titles, and more complex editing.

Geriatric1927 has also become something of an evangelist. In the video entry 'Computing for the Terrified,'[11] Oakley records himself carrying on a conversation over video chat with 'a group of elderly residents living in sheltered accommodation who are receiving instruction into basic computer techniques.' Although we can only hear one side of the conversation, Oakley is clearly reassuring and encouraging them to just 'have a go,' using his own process of self-education as an example. He advises the participants in his workshop to 'just click around' or 'play a simple card game' to get the hang of the mouse until it's 'almost like a third hand,' after which 'all sorts of amazing things will happen,' and not to worry, because 'you really can't break a computer.' In fact, he says, 'you must be prepared to be a child again' – to learn by 'playing around.'

The interesting thing to observe here is how Oakley's videos make his own process of learning explicit through a process of reflection and communication – thus making his knowledge available to his peers. Beyond functional computer literacy, YouTube is a platform for peer learning and knowledge sharing about all kinds of things – guitar-playing, cooking, dancing, and computer games. Videos of players doing in-game stunts,[12] compilations of in-game achievements,[13] or illustrations of how to exploit glitches in games[14] are as much about sharing knowledge as they are about 'showing off' and showcasing one's own competencies. Further, the specific technological and cultural competencies that are required in order to navigate, communicate and innovate within YouTube as a social network, as the example of Geriatric1927 demonstrates, are collectively constructed, taught and learned as part of how the social network develops. This process also takes great patience and a degree of fortitude.

But before we become overly enthusiastic about the possibilities for informal learning and self-education that participation in YouTube makes possible, we should note that the dominance of vlogging in shaping what counts as the means to participate actively in the community may privilege some identities over others. That is, to build an online presence within the YouTube community as a vlogger requires time, patience, and persistence, rather than a more casual mode of engagement with YouTube. It also requires a certain propensity for self-revelation and even self-promotion: ongoing participation as a vlogger requires that you be willing to commit yourself to being visible to the community and, potentially, to the wider public – to put your head on camera and put yourself 'out there.' As much as YouTube supports performative and productive engagement in participatory culture, issues remain about how space can be made for other, quieter forms of participation to be recognized within the YouTube community, and to be properly valued as components of digital literacy elsewhere.

CHAPTER FIVE

YouTube's Cultural Politics

There's no getting away from it: YouTube is a commercial enterprise. But it is also a platform designed to enable cultural participation by ordinary citizens. It is a highly visible example of the broader trend toward uneasy convergences of market and non-market modes of cultural production in the digital environment, where marginal, subcultural, and community-based modes of cultural production are by design incorporated within the commercial logics of major media corporations. As we have already suggested, YouTube's value is partly generated out of the collective creativity and communication of its users and audiences, and its culture has both commercial and community motivations and outcomes. In some ways this situation requires a shift in focus for the cultural politics of the media – when commerce and community are not so easily separated, new versions of old questions arise. Ellie Rennie (2006) discusses this issue in relation to community media, which she describes as functioning historically as both a site of the 'commons' and a site of cultural innovation that operates alongside the market but that is not driven by it. This traditional model of innovation from the margins, Rennie argues, is threatened by the convergence of corporate interests with the Internet: marketization might mean the enclosure, and therefore the failure, of the commons, thereby impacting negatively on media diversity and innovation. Taking Rennie's concerns as a starting point, the fundamental question is whether YouTube's domination of online video distribution, and the market logic behind it, represents a similar threat to the viability of alternative or community media spaces, or alternatively, whether its visibility and accessibility might in some ways actually promote and sustain them.

It is doubtful that YouTube, Inc. ever had the aims of 'community media' as part of its mission to any great extent. It was always first and foremost a commercial enterprise, building an audience for advertising by enabling individual users to share video for personal and entertainment purposes. But we might suggest that it has also turned out to be a *site* of similar opportunities as those offered by community media, not in spite of but *because* of its mainstream commerciality. That is, the commercial drive behind and the hype around YouTube may have produced the possibility of participation in online video culture for a much broader range of participants than before. This idea allows us to shift our concern away from the false opposition between market and non-market culture, toward a concern with the tensions that arise when corporate logics have to contend with the unruly and emergent characteristics of participatory culture, and the limits of YouTube's business model for cultural diversity and global communication.

Following this logic, in this chapter we explore the idea that YouTube is generating public and civic value as an unintended and often unsupported consequence of the practices of its users. If we imagine YouTube in this way then some interesting questions emerge. We ask to what extent the unintentionally produced cultural, civic and social value of YouTube is truly being valued, especially by the company itself; and we explore the implications of public good being created collectively by private individuals via the enabling technology of a company that is responsible for complying with the principles and regulations of corporate responsibility, but which is not necessarily required to prioritize the public interest. The larger in scale and demographic reach of YouTube, the more that is at stake, and the more significant the already-existing tensions between top-down and bottom-up, 'labor' and 'play,' democracy and profiteering, are likely to become.

Everyday Cultural Citizenship and the Cultural Public Sphere

YouTube is big enough, and global enough, to count as a significant mediating mechanism for the cultural public sphere. Beyond the very obvious and much-hyped role YouTube videos and audiences played in the 2008 US Presidential campaign, the ordinary activities of its users, in theory, could constitute practices of cultural citizenship; if they encounter one another under the right conditions, the website is an enabler of encounters with cultural differences and the development of political 'listening' across belief systems and identities. How are these ideas of a cultural public sphere and cultural citizenship connected in theory, and how do they appear to help us explain what YouTube is, and is not, doing in terms of cultural politics?

There is by now a substantial body of work that argues commercial popular culture can sometimes be literally as constitutive of cultural citizenship as the spaces of formal politics, especially for women, queers, and racial or ethnic minorities (Hartley, 1999; Hermes, 2005, 2006; McKee, 2004). Connected to this is the idea that contemporary citizenship is not only a matter of an individual's codified rights and obligations in relation to the state, but also concerns the ways individuals participate in practices and collectivities that form around matters of shared interest, identity or concern. Joke Hermes (2005) suggests notions of citizenship 'can also be used in relation to less formal everyday practices of identity construction, representation, and ideology, and implicit moral obligations and rights' (2005: 4), defining 'cultural citizenship' as:

> the process of bonding and community building, and reflection on that bonding, that is implied in partaking of the text-related practices of reading, consuming, celebrating, and criticizing offered in the realm of (popular) culture. (2005: 10)

Popular cultural texts and practices, she writes, are important because 'they provide much of the wool from which the social tapestry is knit.' Karina Hof (2006: 364) uses these ideas in a study of scrapbooking communities, arguing 'scrapbooking exemplifies how an everyday cultural practice can magnetize and mobilize people through a community of practice.' Participation in both scrapbooking as an individual creative practice and in communities of practice that form around scrapbooking, Hof argues, 'offers a very visible form and forum through which scrappers show what and whom they care about, how they live and where they fit into society at large' (2006: 364) (self-representation as a cultural citizen). Not only that, but such cultural participation also entails the exercising of 'duties and privileges' (the practice of cultural citizenship). This model of cultural citizenship could just as easily apply to the creation, showcasing and discussion of video content in YouTube. William Uricchio (2004: 140) argues that participation in certain P2P (peer-to-peer) communities 'constitutes a form of cultural citizenship, and that the terms of this citizenship have the potential to run head to head with established political citizenship.' Uricchio proposes a model of cultural citizenship that directly incorporates the reconfigured relations between (formerly centralized) cultural production and consumption in participatory culture:

> Community, freed from any necessary relationship to the nation-state, and participation, in the sense of active, then, are two prerequisites for the enactment of cultural citizenship . . . And it is in this context that I want to assert that certain forms of . . . participatory culture . . . in fact constitute sites of cultural citizenship. I refer here particularly to collaborative communities, sites of collective activity that exist thanks only to the creative contributions, sharing, and active participation of their members. (Uricchio, 2004: 148)

Unlike a local community of practice, in YouTube there is also the matter of the relationship between the individual and the 'community' in the face of globalization and cultural difference. Gandy (2002: 458) argues that the 'real digital divide' is the result of a social shaping of new media toward the interests of already powerful social groups, marked by class-specific characteristics, including profound individualization. Michael Tracey (1998: 263) frames this social shaping as a barrier to what has been traditionally understood as a democratic public sphere – creating a mediated social world that is 'profoundly individualistic and definitely not collective, public, shared, or coherent.' Infinite customization and the proliferation of 'niche markets' do not necessarily result in a more democratic participatory culture, regardless of whether the culture is produced by individuals or corporations. However, Nick Stevenson (Stevenson, 2003a, 2003b) argues it is possible to imagine a progressive, cosmopolitan cultural citizenship despite the reality of our increased individualization, if we can imagine a revived model of the public sphere, based on the promotion of sustained opportunities for participation and dialogue, requiring the genuine negotiation of complexity and difference.

The idea that a commercial website organized around entertainment – whatever the source of its 'content' – can contribute to such worthy ideals is not as far fetched as it might at first appear. Indeed, it is because so much of the symbolic material mediated via YouTube originates in the everyday lives of ordinary citizens, or is evaluated, discussed, and curated by them, that YouTube, in theory, represents a site of cosmopolitan cultural citizenship. But the communicative practices that constitute this form of cultural citizenship are more frequently found very far down the 'long tail' from the spectacular, antagonistic and less nuanced 'common culture' of YouTube that was the subject of the previous chapter, where 'intercultural' communication tends to revert to histrionics and a battle between dramatized stereotypes.

Quietly bubbling away under the surface are the kinds of activities that might be recognized by feminist scholars of popular culture as the practices of cultural citizenship – mundane but engaging activities that create spaces for engagement and community-formation. Models of participation that function in this way range from peer-to-peer guitar lessons to 'memes' based around everyday consumer-citizenship, where a large number of YouTube participants respond in video form to questions like 'What's in your fridge?';[1] as well as genuinely empathetic spaces for identity-based communities, such as transgender communities. See, for example, the range of generally supportive, 'educational' and expansive comments and related videos on the hundreds of otherwise unremarkable and narrowly biographical video blog entries returned for the keyword search 'transgender.' It is these meta-texts around the video diaries of transgender people, particularly as they transition, that work to constitute community and at the same time to bring the issues around transgender activism and identity into the public sphere.

Patricia Lange (2007c, n.p.) notes that even though

> people who are unfamiliar with the diary form of video blogging are often critical of this genre, seeing it as self-centered and obsessed with filming micro-events with no particular point or relevance beyond the videomaker's own life . . . many video bloggers argue that it is precisely by putting these intimate moments on the Internet for all to see that a space is created to expose and discuss difficult issues and thereby achieve greater understanding of oneself and others.

Drawing on her ethnographic interviews with (mainly women) videobloggers, Lange argues that 'public access to intimate moments and the discourse surrounding the video artifacts on the Web allow social boundaries and pre-existing assumptions to be questioned and refashioned,' therefore converting the interpersonal and intimate identity work of everyday life to articulate to more 'public' debates around social identities, ethics, and cultural politics. In contrast to the spectacular flame wars between atheists and theists that were frequently a feature of our sample of the most popular content, Lange describes a case in her study, in which 'the quiet, intimate, yet public exploration of feelings about atheism set in motion by a private conversation with a coworker prompted a reconsideration of how personal views may transform into political questions.' In these quiet moments of communication facilitated via, but not contained within, the video blog as 'text,' Lange sees hope for an enrichment of public discourse: 'by being vulnerable and sharing intimate moments and choices, it is possible to promote increased public discourse about formerly uncomfortable, distasteful, or difficult topics in ways that other media and other methods have not.'

This mode of participation is not limited to the videoblog, however. The quoting of traditional media content we discussed in Chapter 3 also constitutes a very ordinary way in which citizens participate in or create the debates Lange identifies. Constructing meaning through redaction can work to serve similar purposes – delineating, articulating, and expressing particular identities and modes of engagement with the world as members of particular communities; sports and anime fandoms provide particularly vibrant examples. Some of the quoted material in our sample featured footage from soccer matches, edited to include pictures of fans, and details of their adventures following certain teams throughout the season. Videos such as these give material form and visibility to the identities of fans as members of a community of fellow enthusiasts. Uploading this material serves as a way for the group to talk among themselves, and to the broader community, using the same media texts that bring them together. The discussions that take place there spill over into other sites of everyday culture, meaning, and identity practice. So too, the uploading of Philippino or Turkish soap opera episodes, divided into pieces to get around YouTube's content limits, can be seen as acts of cultural citizenship akin to the media sharing practices of diasporic communities identified by Cunningham and Nguyen (2000).

YouTube is a potential site of cosmopolitan cultural citizenship – a space in which individuals can represent their identities and perspectives, engage with the self-representations of others, and encounter cultural difference. But access to all the layers of possible participation is limited to a particular segment of the population – those with the motivations, technological competencies, and site-specific cultural capital sufficient to participate at all levels of engagement the network affords. The cultural citizens who have the highest probability of encountering one another are those who engage most deeply with these various layers. This is what is commonly referred to as the 'participation gap' (Jenkins, 2006a: 258; Jenkins *et al.*, 2006), and this is why both digital literacy and inclusive online communities are such important issues for cultural politics. 'Voice' is still unevenly distributed; particularly noticeably in YouTube – a website that is US-dominated demographically to an extent; but whose common culture – at least as represented by our sample – feels culturally US-dominated out of all proportion.

Further, access to voice is no guarantee of an empathetic or engaged audience (Couldry, 2006). The dominant discourses around participatory culture (including the very idea of a gap in participation) appear to frame passive engagement as a kind of lack – continuing to affirm and reward those who speak more than those who listen. Some of the excitement and energy around participatory culture was motivated by the possibility that those of us who had been limited to the role of the 'passive' audience could become producers, and therefore more 'active' participants in the media. While the affordances of the technologies and media forms associated with the participatory turn have increased the range of producers, and undoubtedly moved a significant number of people toward cultural production, continuing to value only those who produce replicates the politics of the previous system. It is important to consider consumption and audience practices as significant modes of participation, rather than as a lack of participation – as in the widespread habit of referring to the online audience as (mere) 'lurkers'. Similarly, it is important to consider the possibility that forms of participation *requiring* original content creation are potentially less inclusive than forms of participation that combine a range of modes of participation (including sharing, commenting, and viewing as well as the contribution of original content). Indeed, Nightingale (2007) suggests that the availability of a *range* of modes of participation, including 'listening' (or viewing) as well as 'speaking', is one explanation for the mass popularity of YouTube and MySpace.

One of the fundamental characteristics of co-creative environments like YouTube is that the participants are all at various times and to varying degrees audiences, producers, editors, distributors, and critics. But the cultural implications of the audience practices that form part of this complexity are not yet well understood. A question for the field of media literacy as it moves forward in the context of participatory culture is how skillful and empathetic reading and listening, especially across difference, might become more central to the politics and pragmatics of new media literacy.

Globalization and Localization

Stewart Butterfield, co-founder of Flickr, once encapsulated the corporate vision for the photo-sharing website in the phrase 'the eyes of the world':

> That can manifest itself as art, or using photos as a means of keeping in touch with friends and family, 'personal publishing' or intimate, small group sharing. It includes 'memory preservation' (the de facto understanding of what drives the photo industry), but it also includes the ephemera that keeps people related to each other: do you like my new haircut? should I buy these shoes? holy smokes – look what I saw on the way to work! It lets you know who's gone where with whom, what the vacation was like, how much the baby grew today, all as it's happening . . . And most dramatically, Flickr gives you a window into things that you might otherwise never see, from the perspective of people that you might otherwise never encounter. (Butterfield, 2006)

Butterfield's explanation links together individual consumption, social intimacy and everyday creativity with global intercultural communication – all based around sharing personal photographs. If Flickr aims to be the 'eyes of the world,' is YouTube the eyes *and* the ears? YouTube is 'global' in the sense that the Internet is – it is accessible from (almost) anywhere in the world, a feature that brings it into conflict with the content filtering and media control frameworks of a number of nations. It is also *globalizing* in that it allows virtual border crossings between the geographical location of producers, distributors and consumers. The discussion that follows considers whether this results in a more cosmopolitan media space or one comprised of a greater number of disconnected niche groups.

In June 2007 YouTube began rolling out a series of localized versions of the website. By mid-2008 there were 'YouTubes' in Germany, Australia, Canada, the United Kingdom, Ireland,

New Zealand, Spain, Mexico, France, Italy, China, Japan, the Netherlands, Poland, Brazil, Russia, Hong Kong, and Taiwan. Upon visiting the YouTube website, users could opt for a localized version by selecting from a localization menu with the options represented by the flags of each country for which a localized version was available. Content was customized for location, returning search results that were deemed more 'relevant' to the user based on their geographic location, as well as providing country-specific video rankings and comments. As at August 2008, users could choose the particular country version they wished to view, but they could also choose a language separately, meaning any country's version of the website could be viewed in any of the available languages. It is also possible to leave the country designation 'global,' the default designation for the United States, which does not have an apparent country-specific designation. However, the existence of this choice might turn out to be temporary or dependent on the platform – the YouTube application for the iPhone 3G at launch provided no such options, and seemed to be locked into displaying content filtered for the device's location.

At the time, this move toward the localization of the website created some strange and problematic conflations of 'language,' geopolitics, and location. Although the press releases announcing the introduction of localization focus on 'personalization,' it seems safe to assume the move was undertaken as much in order to allow the company to more easily strike deals with content providers and advertisers as to offer more relevant videos to its users.[2] While in theory the introduction of languages other than English across YouTube might promote greater diversity of participation by removing some of the US-centricity of the website and ameliorating the language barrier issues for participants who do not have English as a first language, 'language' and 'localization' are actually two separate issues.

In our study, coders were asked to indicate whether each video was in a language other than English, and if so, to identify the language of the video. In our sample of the most popular content, only around 15 percent of the videos were in any language other than English, which is a striking, if not surprising result. The sample was composited on machines based in the United States, and drew always on the 'global' version (also the default version for US-based audiences). Although English appears to be operating as a lingua franca in many areas of web culture (Rose, 2005), non-native speakers of English have for some time now outnumbered native speakers. So while English is now a global language, it is not permanently or inevitably so, and it doesn't simply mean that English-*speakers* have a secure cultural hegemony (see Crystal, 2005). Therefore, the apparent 'dominance' of English is probably not as important as questions about the extent to which YouTube's 'common culture' exhibits and supports genuine cultural diversity.

Community responses to the introduction of localization were sparse and largely indifferent, and protest videos relating to the move were quite difficult to find. The dominant line of complaint could be summed up as, 'Dude, where's my country?' – a complaint that came mainly from people from English-speaking countries such as Australia and Canada. Those who did protest not only resented having to choose between either the UK flag or the US one (which, until uproar prompted the company to revert to a 'globe' symbol, was used to represent the 'default,' global version of the website), but also felt moved to demand a version of YouTube localized for their own countries, in a kind of 'me too-ism.' Indeed, in the period the research for this book was undertaken, the only prominent controversy that came close to addressing the issues of cultural diversity and globalization in relation to company decisions were around YouTube, Inc. composition of a 'Community Council' that only comprised white participants.[3] Even then though, the fact that the 'community council' was also dominated by North Americans appeared to escape the notice of most of the participants in this debate.

In Segev, Ahituv, and Barzilai-Nahon's (2007) comparative study of MSN and Yahoo! homepages across various local markets, they quite presciently argue that it is equally important to be concerned about US website visitors encountering less 'global' content as it is to be concerned about the dominance of local websites with US content. From the point of view of cultural politics, it is questionable whether localization would be a good thing for cosmopolitan cultural citizenship, which requires the genuine encounter with difference. Indeed, under such criteria, because of their 'introverted' mode of engagement with the outside world (Rose, 2005), perhaps US-based YouTube participants need a *globalized* YouTube far more than the rest of the world needs a 'localized' one. While US and other English-speaking users are introverted language users and cultural consumers, Richard Rose argues speakers of languages other than English are generally more cosmopolitan, which, he suggests, adds up to a significant and growing form of 'soft power' in the context of globalization.

Too much personalization, customization and localization may actually turn out to be a bad thing, both for the development of cosmopolitan cultural citizenship and for continued cultural innovation. Localization in particular, may have the effect of filtering out non-US and non-English speaking content for US viewers, and make it decreasingly unnecessary for Western, English-speaking users to encounter cultural difference in their experience of the website. Of course, localization may bring with it easier compliance with particular national legal and regulatory frameworks – a consistent source of corporate headaches for both YouTube and its parent company Google; and may make it easier to attract content partners and advertisers in particular regional markets. Indeed, in some countries with strong local content traditions, such as Korea and China, YouTube has made little impact at all so far, despite aggressive marketing attempts on behalf of the company.[4]

The overall impression is of a company negotiating a range of competing national regulatory structures and corporate demands while at the same time maintaining a brand image based on universal accessibility, and ideologically embedded in a particularly US-centric model of 'free speech.' Tensions arise around the need to control which 'markets' certain content is accessed in (primarily an issue for corporate content providers like music labels and television networks) or to navigate the content regulation and censorship regimes of particular states – for example, to comply with the very strong regulation around hate speech and neo-Nazi imagery in Germany. Increasingly it appears these tensions are resolved through the selective use of content-specific geolocal filters. (See, for example, the discussion at OpenNet Initiative, 2008.) It seems clear that Google, YouTube, corporate content providers, and national governments are quietly enacting a range of content filtering policies, effectively shaping and reshaping the possibilities of YouTube as an influential part of the networked cultural public sphere, but with no real responsibility to disclose the details of, or reasoning behind, these decisions to users. As users, we are generally none the wiser, instead being suddenly confronted by mysteriously inaccessible videos and incomplete search results, accompanied by nothing more than enigmatic messages like 'this video is not available in your country,' or 'a portion of these search results cannot be displayed in accordance with local laws and regulations.'

The Accidental Archive

One of the apparently puzzling things about YouTube is the stark difference between the characteristics of the most popular content and the answer we get to the question 'What do you watch on YouTube?' One thing people often tell us is that they spend hours at a time watching old music videos, half-forgotten TV commercials, or clips from *Sesame Street* – recapturing memories from their childhood or young adulthood, navigating through related videos or keyword searches, often discovering media moments they thought had been lost forever. This points us toward an important and widespread alternative use of YouTube, but one that is less frequently featured in discussions of its implications: the use of YouTube as a cultural archive.

It is possible to exhaust your own capacity for nostalgia before exhausting the possibilities of the vintage material available on

YouTube already. Some major music labels who have channels on YouTube are increasingly adding videos from the vault, and channels such as HBO are uploading old promotional spots and program bumpers, but most of the vintage music videos, documentary films, advertisements, and children's shows that constitute this archive have been made available as the result of hours of painstaking labor, undertaken by the amateur collectors and curators of television who are digitizing VHS tapes in their garages, editing them for upload at YouTube, tagging and describing them, and arranging them into playlists or 'groups.' Even without the contributions of these pro-am collectors, archivists, and curators, whose practices contribute to building YouTube as a cultural archive, it is evolving into one as an unintended consequence of how it is used. Indeed, YouTube's status as an archive is more consistent with YouTube's now-abandoned 'Your Digital Video Repository' tagline than their current provocation to 'Broadcast Yourself.' The collective activities of thousands of users, each with their individual enthusiasms and eclectic interests, are resulting in what is effectively a living archive of contemporary culture from a large and diverse range of sources. In fact, if YouTube remains in existence for long enough, the result will be not only a repository of vintage video content, but something even more significant: a record of contemporary global popular culture (including vernacular and everyday culture) in video form, produced and evaluated according to the logics of cultural value that emerge from the collective choices of the distributed YouTube user community. YouTube is thus evolving into a massive, heterogeneous, but for the most part accidental and disordered, public archive.

This idea of YouTube as an archive has significance for the prospect of widespread popular co-creation of cultural heritage, supplementing the more specifically purposeful and highly specialized practices of state-based cultural archiving institutions like public libraries and museums; or media companies and broadcasters. Writing in a journal devoted to librarianship studies, Karen F. Gracy (2007) considers the implications of YouTube as an unfiltered, bottom-up cultural archive for the role cultural institutions play:

> If cultural institutions no longer muster the same authority to curate collections – and by curate I mean shape them through the activities of acquisition, appraisal, description, deaccessioning, and all the other processes in which such institutions engage – what is their role within society and in regard to cultural heritage? (Gracy, 2007: 184)

So cultural institutions are considering how such developments will impact on their own missions and practices, but less consideration is usually given to the implications of commercial spaces taking on some of the work of cultural institutions without being tied to the same public and state-based responsibilities. Archivist Rick Prelinger (2007) argues that those who have provided the infrastructure which has unexpectedly produced these accidental archives, as in the case of YouTube, are mostly 'blithely unconcerned by [the] questions of persistence, ownership, standards, sustainability, or accountability' that occupy professional archivists and their parent institutions. Because YouTube offers its service based on commercial interests, rather than public ones, there is no obligation to store these data beyond the commercial viability of the company that provides the storage service. Nor is there any straightforward way cultural institutions can re-archive material that shows up on YouTube, because of legal barriers such as copyright law, and YouTube's Terms of Use.

The question of preservation highlights the precariousness of YouTube as a cultural resource – who is going to archive the archive? And what is going to be preserved? YouTube's *value* as a cultural archive is actually a direct result of its unfiltered, disordered, vernacular, and extremely heterogeneous characteristics. Given that, should decisions about what to preserve be subject to the traditional criteria of cultural and historical 'significance,' or does the idea of YouTube as 'bottom-up' cultural archive demand we question the ideological underpinnings of top-down thinking around cultural heritage? These are questions that librarians and information scientists are already actively engaged in considering (see Lloyd, 2007; Shah and Marchionini, 2007; Gracy, 2007), but within cultural and media studies, they have not yet received as much attention as they deserve.

Beyond preservation, one of the most important functions of cultural institutions is to organize, catalogue, interpret, and re-present the archive for public use. But YouTube, in several important ways, is profoundly disordered. As Weinberger points out for other content aggregating sites with a 'flat' architecture like Flickr or del. icio.us (Weinberger, 2007: 100), the way the content is actually arranged and presented on the YouTube website does not determine how that content will be re-aggregated, interpreted, and arranged for display by users. The video content that constitutes this vast archive is not filtered on its way in; it is filtered in use and through repurposing and re-presentation elsewhere. While various strategies are employed by YouTube's editors and website designers to introduce some filters and perform some shaping of this archive (by 'featuring' videos on the front page, or creating blog entries drawing attention to certain kinds of videos), in the context of this vast archive of content, the intermediary and curatorial roles played by users, external bloggers, and existing online communities of interest are far more important. As Gehl (2009) argues, in YouTube the elements required for the collection and curation of a public archive are not organized around this purpose. While YouTube might contribute significant public value as an 'accidental' cultural archive, the question of who is responsible for it, and to what extent these questions are even relevant to a commercial enterprise, have yet to be properly asked, yet alone answered.

Controversies in the YouTube Community

As is the case in other sites of participatory culture (like MMOGs and social network sites), controversies sometimes arise within the self-constituted YouTube community around the uneasy relationship between the company and its users. To borrow from Bruno Latour (2005), such controversies are highly significant and analytically useful events: in the case of YouTube, they reveal the uncertain and contested quality of the power relations between the community and the company, the level of investment these users have in protecting YouTube's attention economy from the intrusions of Big Media, as well as the construction of symbolic boundaries between the YouTubers as a core group of 'lead users' and an imagined 'mass' of ordinary users.

These controversies reveal competing ideas about what YouTube is for – a social network site produced by communities of practice; a chaotic archive of weird, wonderful, and trashy vernacular video; or a distribution platform for branded and Big Media entertainment. Much of the discussion around these controversies centers around changes or perceived changes to the culture of YouTube as it scales up, makes deals with major media players and attempts to create revenue from its constantly evolving business model. In participating in the debates around these controversies, the YouTubers exert an influence on a complex system to which they collectively contribute much of the value, performing and protecting the considerable personal investments they have in the YouTube culture and community.

The activity that occurred around the launch of Oprah Winfrey's YouTube channel in early November 2007 was a particularly good example of the way participants in YouTube's social network use their own video channels to shape and contest the way the culture of YouTube is evolving. The launch was cross-promoted via a 'YouTube special' on the Oprah television show ('YouTube's Greatest Hits With The Billionaire Founders,' 2007), in which a number of the current and all-time most viewed videos and their creators were featured as guest stars. It seemed to commenters that at some stage in that first week, the Oprah channel had been granted the privilege of editing the list of featured videos that appears on the front page of the YouTube website, with the result being that the featured videos that week were predominantly (and approvingly) *about* Oprah in some way. There was an intense and immediate flurry of protest videos, spawning discussion about the implications of this event. One point made by several commentators was that Oprah was importing the convergence of celebrity and control associated with 'big media' into the social media space (by disallowing external embedding, by moderating comments) and therefore ignoring the cultural norms that have developed over the life of the network. The Oprah channel was seen as symptomatic of late-arriving corporate partners exploiting the market in attention that had been produced by earlier, more 'authentic' participants, a situation only exacerbated by YouTube's practice of proactively promoting their partnerships with mainstream media companies and celebrities who hadn't done the 'hard yards' in the subculture.

The blog devoted to YouTube, *YouTube Stars*,[5] summed up the themes of the debates that occurred around this event:

> The YouTube community has reacted with ambivalence to Oprah's new channel. Some think it will bring new viewers for everyone's videos. But others object to Oprah's apparent 'one-way conversation' – she seems to want to advertise to us without accepting feedback. It has also been lamented that the 'golden age' of YouTube is over. With the corporate accounts racking up lots of viewers, it's hard to get on the most discussed or most viewed lists without resorting to histrionics and sensationalism. YouTube seemed more like a community of videomakers before 'partners' came on to advertise to us. But, all this was inevitable. YouTube was spending millions on the computer power and bandwidth necessary to provide this free service to the uploaders and viewers of the thousands of new videos posted weekly on the website.

In 'Noprah,'[6] an entry from his humorous vlog, star YouTuber Nalts responded to the Oprah 'YouTube special' and her related move to establish a channel on YouTube. Nalts complained about the 'same old' videos, like the 'skateboarding dog,' being used by 'Big Media' to represent YouTube. He voiced his irritation with Big Media not understanding the YouTube 'community,' as well as Oprah's own channel not allowing comments. Renetto, another A-list YouTuber and self-styled community leader, sarcastically commented that it was a good thing that Oprah got featured on the front page because, clearly, 'she has trouble broadcasting herself.'[7]

At around the same time, popular British vlogger Paperlilies argued in an entry entitled 'RIP the Golden Age of YouTube,'[8] that the entrance of corporate players had produced a 'crazy playing field.' Asserting that her own videos are made 'in [her] bedroom,' 'using iMovie,' she proposed that YouTube needed to look at introducing new ways for visitors to navigate and find content that would allow people to find 'good' user-created content. She went on to express anxiety about the impact on the cultural ecology of YouTube of the company's recent success in attracting corporate partners:

> It felt like it was a community and it doesn't feel like that anymore. It feels like we're living in a TV channel and no-one's looking at us, we're just being trodden all over by corporate people who don't give a shit about the people who make videos.

There was a palpable sense of betrayal in these entries, along with the idea the investment of time and effort the YouTube community has put in has gone unrewarded. This is not just a rights-based complaint motivated by jealousy or the loss of attention. Comments like these exhibit an ethic of care for the 'YouTube-ness' of YouTube, and an aspiration to preserve the unique and diverse flavor of 'bottom-up' participation. For Paperlilies and other 'lead' YouTubers, this is an issue of cultural diversity and sustainability, as much as one of mutual responsibility. She says, addressing the company:

> You've got the corporate thing now, you've got it down pat. Everyone wants to be on YouTube and that's great. But now you've got to go back to those people who made YouTube what it is, and promote them. Because a lot of people are feeling neglected by YouTube. And the site that they grew to love last summer is no more. Now we have just another TV channel that happens to be on the Internet. And I don't like that.

Whereas it used to be that 'creative' or 'well-made' videos could get a 'huge amount of views,' she said, now 'sensationalist' videos or those appealing to the 'lowest common denominator' get a lot of views, providing what the 'mainstream media' was providing before the emergence of YouTube. 'Creativity' (understood as innovative user-created content) is 'harder to find' the more content there is.

At the same time, however, Blunty, another very well-known YouTuber, expressed skepticism about the extent of the threat 'real celebrities' represent. He pointed out that the same debates occurred when Paris Hilton and P. Diddy got YouTube channels, occurrences which provoked a great deal of anxiety that later turned out to be unwarranted: 'Neither P. Diddy nor Paris Hilton really affected the YouTube community in any way, shape or form.' Blunty also argued that Oprah's cross-promotion of her own YouTube presence would have the unintended consequence of bringing new audiences, not to the Oprah brand, but also to *user-created* YouTube content. In the end, Oprah is 'just another YouTuber,' he concludes, but one who may significantly expand the audience, hence benefiting the community as a whole; and, in fact, the protest videos themselves could be seen as a way of cashing in on the Oprah brand, diverting the resultant attention back toward the YouTubers themselves.

The controversy around Oprah's entrance to YouTube, then, functioned partly as an opportunity for the community to explicitly reflect on, take stock of, and activate around the terms of participation within which they work. These videos were also part of a much longer-term and more widespread pattern of community 'protest' videos, frequently led by the more well-known YouTubers. In her vlog entry entitled 'YouTube is NOT involved with the Community,' xgobobeanx discussed a number of perceived inadequacies and inequities in YouTube's community management practices. Her description of the video expressed irritation that 'YouTube does not answer emails and that anyone can flag a video with out any notice or explanation. Why do partners get away with so much?' Much of the argument is grounded in a separation between (commercial) partners on the one hand, and 'the community' (non-corporate 'YouTubers') on the other. The importance of this distinction is also illustrated by some of the counter-tactics employed by the YouTube community to gain some control over the public landscape of the website. For example, the website *YouTube Stars* regularly publishes a chart of the 'Non Corporate Top 100' YouTube videos, which is similar to YouTube's Most Viewed page, but with all content uploaded by known corporate partners filtered out.[9]

This resistance to the perceived commercial appropriation of grass-roots enterprise is not unique to YouTube, of course. It is very similar to the perception of 'appropriation' or 'selling out' that have been so well documented in relation to music subcultures and scenes that go from being marginal to the mainstream (see, for example, Schilt, 2003, on the Riot Grrrl phenomenon in the 1990s). Protesting, parodying, or participating in the turbulence around the perceived transformation of YouTube from DIY free-for-all to corporate media platform is a way of performing insider knowledge and expertise. The discourse that takes places around these controversies reveals the tensions between the 'active' participants, or 'core users,' who play by the rules that have been collectively established over time by the user community, and those who, according to the perceptions of the YouTubers, contribute to the erosion of the cultural value and integrity of the service by disregarding those norms: haters (who haven't uploaded their own videos but leave abusive comments in the discussion threads of other users' videos); big media players (like Oprah) who assume the privileges of cultural authority without earning them on the ground. But these issues cannot simply be reduced to 'early adopters' feeling that the mainstream is taking over. These discussions and controversies actually reveal the shared but implicit understanding of the social contract between the YouTubers and YouTube, Inc. This implicit understanding might only be made explicit once it appears to be disrupted by new developments (like the Oprah channel), at which time discourses of entitlement, fairness, and even labor emerge.

As well as revealing the emerging politics of the relationships between the YouTube user community, YouTube Inc., and big media organizations, the controversies and debates that can be observed via YouTube vlog entries also concern the norms of behavior within the social network itself. It is well known (if some-times exaggerated) that there are issues in YouTube with abusive comments, exacerbated by anonymity (so that there are few dis-incentives to behave badly) and scale (so that it becomes difficult to keep up with policing and moderating comments). As demon-strated by the relatively recent introduction of moderation into the commenting policy of the very popular weblog BoingBoing, and the very complicated policies surrounding the discussion and editing of Wikipedia entries, it is possible to deal with 'trolls' at an institutional level, as long as an appropriately sophisticated approach is taken to balancing free communication with the quality of the website as a communicative space. But to an extent, the apparently anti-social communicative practices of trolls and haters have already become normalized in the cultural system of YouTube, at least for the most popular videos – in fact, we might say that the comments section of any highly popular video's page is a playspace for the audience as much as it is a means of the uploader getting feedback. Many prominent YouTubers express reluctance to moderate or ban comments because those kinds of controls are counter to the ethos of openness that supposedly distinguishes participatory culture. Lange (2007a) explains that dealing with the 'haters' – negative and often personally offen-sive commenters – is part of the YouTube experience for those who participate in YouTube as a social network, and something YouTubers accept as part of the game, taking the bad with the good. Learning how to 'manage' trolls, both practically and emo-tionally, is one of the core competencies required for effective or enjoyable participation.

However, the community also finds its own ways of negotiating and shaping the social norms of the network. In the collaborative video 'Being a Chick on YouTube,'[10] a male and female YouTuber discussed the implications of the sexist and often abusive com-ments that prominent female YouTubers have to contend with. The video demonstrates a sophisticated knowledge of the issue – rather than moralizing about it, the two participants in the video discussed the possible negative impact of this culture of sexism on the participation rates of female vloggers. Cleverly, it addressed the assumed motivations of the male audience, arguing that the development of an overly masculinist and sexist culture among the YouTube community would result in a scarcity of female YouTubers with whom to interact. This is a good example of how YouTubers are attempting to shape social norms and reflexively negotiate the ethics of online behavior, operating from a position of grounded, insider knowledge, making it more likely that these interventions would be effective than the top-down enforcement of new regulations would be.

The other site of conflict and antagonism in YouTube as a social network is the 'flame war' or 'YouTube drama'– which should be thought of separately from the general carelessness or mischief-making of casual commenters. These events occur when a flurry of video posts clusters around an internal 'controversy' or an antagonistic debate between one or more YouTubers. They can sometimes be based around controversial debates (especially religion, atheism, or politics). But quite often they appear as face-offs between YouTube stars based around the internal politics and power plays of the YouTube community itself. These short-lived, but very intense, community events are often engaged in playfully – they function as entertainment as much as debates and discussions. Indeed, flame wars can be thought of as ludic events: structured games that are part of the fun of participating in the social network.

A good example of this from the period in which our content survey took place was the controversy over prominent user LisaNova allegedly 'spamming' others with comments in order to attract audiences to her channel. It was quite evident that as part of the controversy playing itself out, the trolling, hating, and parodying became spectacle in themselves. The LisaNova flame war also revealed the internal tensions between the very small number of YouTubers who have become partners (and therefore share in the advertising revenue generated on the website), and the larger group of core YouTubers. The occasional antagonisms between 'A-list' YouTubers and the rest of the 'core' user group is partly a result of the monetization of popularity; the success of the YouTube 'stars' is an element of the perception that YouTube is evolving from a community-driven platform to a more mainstream, commercial space.

At issue in these controversies is the extent to which YouTubers (whether partners or not) have an influence on the future of the community in which they have so much investment. Most significantly, they provide an indication of the competing logics of expertise, authority, and value that are at work within YouTube as a cultural space. The controversies also help us to understand how participation in this self-constituted YouTube 'community' relies on various forms of vernacular expertise, combining a critical and literate understanding of the 'attention economy' and the affordances of the network with the ability to navigate the social and cultural norms of the community.

Despite its internal antagonisms, it is YouTube's social network, produced out of interactions between participants via their videos, that provides the environment in which new literacies, new cultural forms, and new social practices – situated in and appropriate to the culture of user-created online video – are 'originated,' 'adopted,' and 'retained' (Potts *et al.*, 2008a). It is the participants in YouTube's social network who are producing much of YouTube's cultural, social, and economic value.

In participatory culture more broadly, any platform's capacity to produce value relies on the active involvement of communities of co-creative users. In fact, platform providers like YouTube are no longer only in the 'media' business; they now are also in the social network business. In the context of games, Humphreys (2005b) argues that platform providers currently have a faltering understanding of this new role as community managers; certainly, it is unclear whether YouTube Inc. is fully committed to the responsibilities as well as the benefits that flow from its role as patron for the creative and collaborative work of its core users – the work that actually produces YouTube *as* a community.

As Jarrett (2008) argues, heavy-handed, top-down community 'management,' especially when designed to placate advertisers rather than to promote a welcoming environment for participation and user-led innovation, would run counter to the self-forming dynamics that have built YouTube as a community, but both the company and the community that co-creates its value would benefit from developing more sophisticated models of community-led governance and measures of 'popularity'; and more responsiveness to user-led innovation. If YouTube is to become culturally diverse, creative, and innovative (and therefore sustainable), then YouTube Inc., along with other 'patrons' of co-creative media, needs to take the collective agency of its core users very seriously indeed.

CHAPTER SIX

YouTube's Uncertain Futures

Who's Sorry Now?

There were two hybrid media events that brought Australia to the attention of the world's media in the months leading up to the writing of this book. While one of them is apparently trivial and the other momentous, the very different ways that each of them moved through YouTube in connection with the mainstream media can be used to productively think through some of the possible futures of participatory culture.

In January 2008, Melbourne teenager Corey Delaney made headlines for the mayhem caused when a party he hosted while his parents were out of town, and which he infamously advertised on MySpace, got out of control (Hastie, 2008; Hughes, 2008). It made news in the mainstream media because it hit all the right targets – habitual moral anxiety around youth, connected to an equally habitual anxiety about the narcissism and exhibitionism associated with online social networks like MySpace. Delaney's outrageously unrepentant on-camera behavior when he was interviewed following the event landed him in hot water with the host of a tabloid current affairs show, who attempted to play the 'moral guardian' role, placing him in the counterpart role of the sheepishly guilty party. This was a role Delaney famously refused, steadfastly denying that television current affairs (and by extension, the mainstream media) had any more authority than the legions of YouTube users and MySpace members who, he appeared to knowingly predict, would take enormous mischievous delight in his continued defiance (Ramadge, 2008). And delight they did: mischief followed upon mischief, as clips of his famous refusal to obediently remove his sunglasses and apologize on camera circulated with wild popularity on the web, and particularly on YouTube. Video parodies and image macros proliferated in a matter of days; websites sardonically dedicated to the teenage 'party planner' appeared, often focusing on Corey's now-infamous yellow sunglasses or mashing up celebrity photographs with Corey-related slogans like 'It wasn't me.' Yet another website featured a game allowing visitors to slap some sense into the rogue teenager. Since Delaney's original MySpace page had been removed, and presumably in full knowledge the mainstream media would be looking forward to include it as part of their coverage of the event and ensuing uproar, Random Brainwave's 'John Surname' created a fake MySpace page, complete with a fabricated video masquerading as the original party invitation.[1] Adding insult to news media's injury, those in the know about the prank were delighted when the UK's Channel 4 News aired the fake invitation video as part of their coverage of the scandal.[2] On YouTube, an amplification of the feedback loop between the event, its ongoing life in web culture, and the mainstream media was created as Fox News added the clips to their YouTube channel 'The Blast,'[3] bringing the phenomenon to the attention of the wider US audience.

On the one hand, this event shows how out-of-step the dominant media, especially commercial current affairs programs, are with the temporalities, in-jokes, and cultural repertoires of participatory culture. On the other, it demonstrates the extent to which participants in MySpace and YouTube are sufficiently literate in both the discourses (of youth, risk, and moral panic) and the format of current affairs to invert those discourses and mobilize them using the rapid spreadability of their own mediated social networks. The mischief-making around the event (like the spoof MySpace page) reveals and exploits this at great speed via the affordances of the network of participatory media platforms. The ethic behind all of this, however, like Delaney's party itself and the mischievous swarming actions of the Anonymous message-board multitude, adds up to little more than 'mischief for mischief's sake.'[4]

An entirely different kind of national media event occurred on 13 February 2008. This was the day on which the Australian Prime Minister opened parliament with an official apology to Australia's Indigenous people, and the Stolen Generation in particular.[5] It was an event that had been centuries in the making and was more than a decade overdue. It had been one of the hottest issues in Australian public life in previous elections and, other than the Federal election a few months earlier, it was arguably one of the most important, widely shared common experiences in the Australian cultural public sphere. In itself, the speech was not only an act of 'speaking,' but also one of *listening*, in the sense that a meaningful official apology would not have been possible without an empathetic incorporation of the hundreds of stories of lives affected by the removal policies of previous governments; stories that had emerged over the previous decades and that were finally given the media space they deserved as the official event drew closer. When the day came, it was broadcast live from Parliament House on the television service of the Australian national broadcaster, the Australian Broadcasting Corporation (ABC).

Ironically, on the eve of the official apology, the top search result for the combination of the keywords 'Australia' and 'sorry' was a clip from the original *A Current Affair* segment showing Corey Delaney's refusal to apologize for his behavior. Eventually the full ABC broadcast was uploaded to YouTube and by the end of the day had received a couple of hundred views. Slowly over the next 24–48 hours the Most Viewed pages of YouTube Australia began to fill with related videos. The kinds of videos that were uploaded (and with which audiences engaged) in response to the occasion collectively provide a fairly good summary of YouTube's diverse uses in general. They included straight uploads of the broadcast for the benefit of people who missed it or to record it for posterity; clips of the 'best bits' of the broadcast, providing the 'quotes' and 'catch-up' functions discussed in Chapter 3; a range of user-created videos using the audio of the speech and remixing it with users' own text-based commentaries and images in order to express individual perspectives and emotional reactions to the event; as well as the inevitable vlog entries offering personal perspectives and opinions on the apology. The text comments on these videos reflect the specific culture of political engagement in YouTube – they were generally characterized by very emotive, hyperbolic 'for-or-against' rhetoric, where raw racism was countered by equally raw moralizing. More informed, nuanced, or deliberative perspectives struggled for space.

These two media events – both of which made a significant impact within the culture of YouTube in symbiosis with the mainstream media – lead to two very different visions of participatory culture. Each of them represents a particular 'frequency of public writing' (Hartley, 2008a) – on the one hand, playful subversion with no purpose but exhibiting the awesome speed and creativity of 'viral' web culture; on the other, a cultural public sphere where conversations, self-mediated representation, and encounters with difference (which can be antagonistic and deaf to the other as much as they can be structured on mutual respect) can occur on popular terms, and yet with noticeably less dynamism and independence from official public culture than 'viral' culture exhibits. But both of these versions of participatory culture are extremely challenging to the Habermasian normative model of the public sphere (Habermas, 1989), which is reliant on critical-rational debate and deliberation; rather than the playfulness and affect that characterize the 'common culture' of YouTube.

The questions that confront us now are about what comes next: whether or not the future of participatory culture can accommodate increasing diversity and breadth of participation, and the extent to which such issues can be made to matter to corporate futures. More specifically, how might the future of YouTube as a commercial enterprise actually be bound up with the politics of participatory culture?

YouTube launched without knowing exactly what it was for, and arguably it is this under-determination that explains the scale and diversity of its uses today. YouTube is a large enough entity, and loosely enough managed, that it can almost be whatever its various participants want it to be. In its continued drive toward a monopoly on online video sharing, YouTube practices a sort of light-touch governance – the rules and permissions that operate on the website are 'just enough' to enable all the uses that take place without necessarily shutting down other possibilites. It has been successful so far precisely because it does not seem to be targeting one particular use or market; and unlike some of the other video-sharing sites, YouTube doesn't appear to be pursuing large media producers entirely *at the expense of* the user community. But at the same time, it is this openness, scale, and diversity that are primarily responsible for the ongoing and escalating conflicts around the meanings, uses, and possible futures of YouTube.

One of the biggest issues for YouTube's future is sustainable growth. A core challenge will be to find a balance between mass popularization (which YouTube has achieved, at least for the moment), innovation, and sustainability (which requires long-term investment and a stable and socially functioning community). Further, the new economics of value co-creation bring with them new relationships of power and responsibility between users and platform providers, which platform providers would be wise to cultivate and protect. YouTube, like all enterprises that rely on user co-creation, will need to find ways to maintain its scale and rate of growth while supporting cultural and aesthetic diversity, and respecting the agency of the communities of users who work to produce its various forms of value – whether economic, cultural, or social.

Recently there have been indications YouTube has begun to concentrate some of the energy it puts into rolling out new features for propagating the social network, rather than just the scale of the website. The homepage has recently been redesigned, for example, so that upon logging in users encounter content related to their social network (subscriptions and friends) and past viewing behavior (recommended videos), rather than the most viewed content. The rhetoric in YouTube's public relations materials appears to indicate that future directions are designed to retain visitors, to strengthen the website's stickiness, and entice users to log in and build relationships with the website, as well as a desire to encourage advertisers to work *within* YouTube rather than just placing advertisements *on* YouTube.[6] These hints gesture toward an ethos more consistent with the practices of YouTube's social core, emphasizing conversation and community over broadcasting.

But in some respects it seems community tools are added almost as an afterthought, long after the community themselves have created solutions, as we discussed in Chapter 4. YouTube launched community 'help' forums in July 2008,[7] for example, before which the website provided very few onsite tools for participants to discuss or share ideas with each other. These conversations took place elsewhere – in forums maintained by users, on blog postings, and more significantly, in videos users posted to each other. That users sought to help themselves where no other help was available should come as no real surprise; what should be surprising is that it took YouTube, Inc. so long to provide effective support for the user community on which the enterprise relies so heavily.

At the same time, the company continues to court big media partners, increase advertising presence, and feature sponsored content on the front page. As a result of these partnerships, YouTube is under increasing pressure to 'manage' the community and 'institute' social norms more palatable to the public and the advertisers. For Kylie Jarrett (2008), this is what produces the corporate conflict between the slogan 'Broadcast Yourself' and the trademark symbol attached to it. Jarrett argues that 'for users whose engagement with YouTube has been defined by the primacy of community, an over-reliance on professional, corporate content is likely to damage the all-important goodwill of the YouTube brand' (Jarrett, 2008: 138).

While the company appears to recognize that 'the anarchic, self-organizing systems that have historically constituted YouTube are a fundamental and financially significant component of the site-as-experience and the site-as-business,' and that therefore, 'to damage the community is to damage the company,' 'the sustainability of this laissez faire position, and consequently the future of

YouTube, is under threat by the very success these mechanisms have produced' (Jarrett, 2008: 137). The extent of this threat is evidenced by reports that, since the Viacom lawsuit commenced, Google has restricted ad sales to videos 'that have been posted or approved by media companies and other partners' (Delaney, 2008), – as little as 4 percent of uploaders. Even before this, however, YouTube has had to contend with a generally conservative advertising industry, which has complained about the lack of content guaranteed to be inoffensive enough for them to run advertising against (Delaney, 2008).

YouTube currently dominates online video, and its share of the market is still growing (Schonfield, 2008), but there is no guarantee that this market dominance is secure. A longer-lasting consequence of the moment of YouTube is a certain degree of dominance over the *idea* of what a video-sharing website should look like, and how it should work. New video-sharing sites intended for niche or alternative communities often end up emulating the look of YouTube, or even somewhat self-defeatingly announcing they will be 'The YouTube for . . . [something else],' without due consideration, it seems, for either how they might design a video-sharing website that can best serve their community, or how YouTube necessarily fails to do so. Examples include TeacherTube, a clone of YouTube for educators,[8] and Story Circles, a dedicated website for sharing community digital stories. Both are almost identical to YouTube in their layout and information architecture (e.g. presenting the Most Viewed and Most Recent videos on the front page).[9]

This is a good moment to remember that YouTube is by no means the only online video service available. There is a range of visions of what online video should be for – from the carefully controlled big media sites that make television content available for free at high quality through platforms like Hulu, to dedicated social networking sites such as Stickam, Seesmic, and 12seconds; from non US-bases services such as DailyMotion and Tudou to platforms specifically designed to support 'high-quality' user-created content like Revver and blip.tv. Each of these sites comes with its own business models, IP arrangements, and contracts with users, each providing services that mirror a particular niche use of YouTube. The hugely popular alternatives to YouTube in parts of the world with very strong local content traditions, particularly China and South Korea, hint at the limits of YouTube's potential as a 'global' service.

Although commercial platforms like YouTube have popularized user-created content, it is fast becoming a feature of the activities of not-for-profit institutions such as public service broadcasters, libraries, and museums as well. However tentatively, these institutions of 'official' culture are incorporating many of the cultural practices and social arrangements of the so-called Web 2.0 business models – user-created content, user-led innovation, and greater porosity to other online services. Through a variety of programming and content strategies, these institutions are integrating participatory culture in ways that befit their remits or charters, such as by promoting the value of 'ordinary' people's experiences and stories as valid forms of public knowledge. Examples from the US, the UK, and Australia include the integration of user-contributed material and narratives in the extended platform for Ken Burns' social history *The War*; the BBC Capture Wales Digital Storytelling program and its offshoots throughout England and Northern Ireland; and the National Library of Australia's integration of Flickr groups and creative commons licensing within its online digital image library PictureAustralia. All these developments serve to remind us of the limits of the extent to which any one social network or user-created content service can achieve a true monopoly.

Above all, what the moment of YouTube highlights is the uncertainty surrounding the future of participatory culture, and the complexity arising from the intersection of various changing and competing ideas about what digital media are, or could be, for. Researchers, practitioners, and critics have an important role to play in thinking through the implications of the current period of turbulence for the future of our media and culture, and suggesting alternative possibilities. Through imagining and contesting these possible futures, criticism, commentary, and cultural practice help to create and contest reality, alongside more dominant discourses on digital technologies and user-created content that come from the business world, from the mainstream media, and from governments.

In making an argument about what they call the 'performativity' of social science research methods, Law and Urry (2004) leave us with a relevant provocation, one that does not apply only to social scientists. The question, they say, is:

> Which realities? Which do we want to help to make more real, and which less real? How do we want to interfere (because interfere we will, one way or another)?' (Law and Urry, 2004: 404)

The present and future 'realities' of participatory culture are not under the control of any one group of interests – whether those of the big industry players like Viacom and Google, or of ordinary citizens and audiences. Through each act of participation or attempted influence, whether in YouTube or elsewhere, participatory culture is being co-created every day, by vloggers, marketers, artists, audiences, lawyers, designers, critics, educators, librarians, journalists, technologists, entrepreneurs – and even academics. Some of these participants have more power, ownership, and control over that reality than others, but the question for all of us is the same. How do we want to interfere?

What Happened Before YouTube

Henry Jenkins

> Until now we have only reappropriated speech in the service of revolutionary movements, crises, cures, exceptional acts of creation. What would a normal, calm, established appropriation of speech be like? (Pierre Levy, 1997)

> Over the next 50 years we will witness an explosion of access and production and distribution of video by communities that could not earlier afford to produce video in their homes, schools, and offices. Just as desktop publishing gave consumers the power of the printing press on their desks (but it took the internet to make everyone a publisher since without it the distribution channel was lacking), and digital audio samplers gave birth to a whole new genre and population of music makers, computational video technology will enable these and new communities to make video a part of their daily communication. (Marc Davis, 1997)

Much written about YouTube assumes that it is unprecedented. After all, no one could have predicted what would happen if everyday people were able to seize the means of cultural production and distribution. Seemingly much of the press (and a fair number of academics) can't seem to remember what happened before YouTube.

There is much that *is* new about YouTube but there is also much that is old. YouTube has a history which extends beyond October 2006 when Google purchased YouTube for $1.65 billion or even June 2005 when the website launched. Much that is written about YouTube implies that the availability of Web 2.0 technologies has enabled the growth of participatory cultures. I would argue the opposite is also true: the emergence of participatory cultures of all kinds over the past several decades paved the way for the early embrace, quick adoption, and diverse use of such platforms.

What is revolutionary about YouTube is that it constitutes, in Levy's terms, 'a normal, calm, established appropriation of speech,' a site where mass media is quoted and redeployed, home media gains public access, and various subcultures produce and share media. It is astonishing that YouTube is so routinely referenced by mass media and so regularly deployed by people we know. Web 2.0 companies like to imagine that they create communities around its brands, products, and services, but corporations rarely create communities; companies court pre-existing communities with their own traditions, their own values and norms, their own hierarchies, their own practices, and their own leadership. YouTube has become the home port for lip-syncers, karaoke singers, trainspotters, birdwatchers, skateboarders, hip hoppers, small time wrestling federations, educators, third wave feminists, churches, proud parents, poetry slammers, gamers, fans, Ron Paul supporters, human rights activists, collectors, hobbyists, and each of these groups has a longer history of media production.

If YouTube seems to have sprung up overnight, it is because so many groups were ready for something like YouTube; they already had communities of practice that supported the production of DIY media, already evolved video genres and built social networks through which such videos could flow. YouTube may represent the epicenter of today's participatory culture but it doesn't represent its origin point for any of the cultural practices people associate with it.

Garage Cinema and the 'Do-It-Yourself Newsroom'

People had been predicting something like YouTube a good decade before it actually hit critical mass. Marc Davis (1997) talked about the coming wave of 'garage cinema,' drawing an analogy to the garage bands associated with Punk Rock:

> Changes in technology will bring about a merging of independent video producers and home video makers into a broad and active market sector . . . When the tools and infrastructure are

in place to enable cheap and effective home use of video annotation, retrieval and repurposing tools, the garages of the world will be the site of the 'New New Hollywood' creating hundreds of millions of channels of video content. The conditions of production and use will have changed such that a large group of amateurs and home users will be regularly making video that can compete in the information marketplace of networked computers. (Davis, 1997: 48)

Like so many other digital revolutionaries, Davis imagines a decentralized system of distribution, one with many channels, rather than a shared platform like YouTube.

Writing in 1997, *Mondo 2000* editor in chief R. U. Sirius (The Web), predicted, ultimately:

anybody will be able to have their own multimedia broadcasting operation on the web. Any time, any day, we'll be able to watch John and Midge down the street eating dinner or Lisa and Frank and Joe in the house on the corner having sex. Sure the audience for most of these things will be small. (In the future, everybody will be famous to 15 people.) (Sirius, 1997: 37)

Gareth Branwyn's 1997 book, *Jamming the Media*, brought together zines, digital sampling, shareware computing, web publishing, culture jamming, cable access activism, and various 'media pranks and art hacks,' seeing them all as means of a democratizing channels of communication:

As technology travels along inevitable trajectories towards 'cheaper, faster, better' it's putting powerful communications technologies into the hands of greater numbers of people ... A new form of media is growing up in cyberspace, a global do-it-yourself newsroom and cultural salon where individuals simultaneously create and consume news and information, blurring the distinction between publisher, reporter, and reader. (Branwyn, 1997: 14)

These predictions of 'garage cinema,' a 'do-it-yourself newsroom,' or bedroom television networks were consistent with the zine culture which Stephen Duncombe (1997) was documenting in *Notes from Underground* that same year:

> In an era marked by the rapid centralization of corporate media,
> zines are independent and localized, coming out of cities, sub-
> urbs, and small towns across the USA, assembled on kitchen
> tables. They celebrate the everyperson in a world of celebrity . . .
> Rejecting the corporate dream of an atomized population broken
> down into discrete and instrumental target markets, zine writers
> form networks and forge communities around diverse identities
> and interests. (Duncombe, 1997: 2)

Such zines were part of the political and cultural avant garde of
the 1970s and 1980s, closely tied to the growth of punk rock and
the emergence of Riot Grrl feminism, yet they were also part of
a much larger history of amateur publishing, which in the case
of the science fiction fan community, could be traced back to the
1920s (Ross, 1991). There was an amateur press association in
the United States as early as the late nineteenth century when
people were creating periodicals on toy printing presses (Petrik,
1992). And these Do-It-Yourself impulses spilled over from print
zines to include the production and circulation of mix tapes and
home videos, as Cynthia Conti (2001) suggests in her case study
of Le Tigre, an important feminist media collective.

Fred Turner (2006) has argued that the modern cyberculture
can trace its roots back to the cultural practices of the cyberculture of the 1960s, including people's radio, early video activism,
underground newspapers and comics, all efforts to deploy low
cost media tools and practices toward alternative ends. Many early
netizens explicitly embraced the value of participatory culture.
Many of these early prophets would recognize YouTube's amateur
media makers as the culmination of their earlier hopes and a vali-
dation of their predictions. In 1997, it was much easier to imagine
large numbers of amateurs producing media than it was to imagine large numbers of people consuming amateur content. In that
same 1997 exchange, Douglas Rushkoff (The Web) argued,

> Right now, the web is a place where everyone is broadcasting yet
> no one is receiving. That's the scam: create a place where every-
> one can vent the pent-up broadcasting urge, when there's very
> little urge to see what the others are saying.

Consider the contrast between R. U. Sirius's future where everyone is famous to fifteen people and the current reality where at least some amateur videos are drawing a million hits. Neither Rushkoff nor Sirius anticipated the scale on which YouTube now operates or the way mass media channels amplify its impact. The rhetoric of digital revolution assumed new media would displace the old, whereas YouTube exemplifies a convergence culture (Jenkins, 2006a) with its complex interactions and collaborations between corporate and grassroots media.

In her book, *Reel Families: A Social History of Amateur Film*, Patricia R. Zimmermann (1995) contrasts the ideals of earlier generations of do-it-yourself filmmakers who saw amateur production as a means of diversifying the commercial sector with the reality that most amateurs produced home movies with little or no chance of larger distribution. One might, for example, see the roots of videoblogging in what teenage avant garde artist Sadie Benning did with her Fischer-Price pixelvision camera: 'Her camera plunges into the subversive and hidden cracks of family life, the places behind the closed doors of a teenager's bedroom, where sexual fantasies and social imagination are debunked and reinvented' (Zimmermann, 1995: 154). What happens when Benning is not unique in confessing her innermost thoughts into a handheld camera, but one among thousands of teens, all sharing their angst via YouTube? YouTube does not so much change the conditions of production as it alters the contexts of circulation and reception: Such works now reach a larger public via its channels of distribution; there are systems of criticism which focus attention on interesting and emerging works; there are people willing to seek out and engage with noncommercial content; and consumers are conversing with each other by producing videos.

Yet, many of those earlier advocates remain skeptical that a commercially owned and operated platform can enable the kinds of alternative politics once associated with the DIY movement. Here's independent filmmaker Alex Juhasz (in Jenkins, 2008a):

My concern is that the counter-cultural, anti-normative, critical, or political impulses behind the term (as it came out of punk, for instance), drop out of the picture – just as they do in most DIY YouTube video – when access to technology occurs outside other liberating forces. I believe that for engagements with the media to be truly transformative, the fact of expanded access to its production and exhibition is only one in a set of necessary conditions that also include a critique, a goal, a community, and a context.

If we want to see a more 'democratic' culture, Juhasz argues, we need to explore what mechanisms might encouraged greater diversity in who participates, whose work gets seen, and what gets valued. More optimistically, human rights activist Ethan Zuckerman argues that any platform sufficiently powerful to enable the distribution of cute cat pictures can also be deployed to bring down a government under the right circumstances. Right now, people are learning how to produce, upload and circulate content. What happens next is up to us.

The Gathering of the Clans

In his book, *The Wealth of Networks*, Yochai Benkler (2006) discusses how shifts in the 'information economy' are allowing 'diversely motivated' groups and individuals greater ability to generate and circulate ideas. While we may safely ascribe some kind of commercial motivation for most of the content produced and distributed by mass media, no such shared agenda shapes the production and distribution of grassroots media. *The Wealth of Networks* describes network culture as the intermingling between commercial, nonprofit, governmental, educational, and amateur modes of cultural production. In this new network culture, with its lowered costs of production and distribution, participants are not 'constrained to organize their relationship through a price system or in traditional hierarchical models of social and economic organization' (Benkler, 2006: 8).

YouTube is a shared space where many different cultural flows intersect and 'diversely motivated' media producers brush against each other. Innovations spread rapidly in such a context as experiments within one community spill over into others; groups which might otherwise have had little or no contact are generating new hybrid models of cultural politics which depend on temporary and tactical alliances between interests. We might extend Benkler's concept of a network culture to describe not only one where these forms co-exist through the same media platform but also one where the lines between them start to blur, where it becomes increasingly difficult to tell where one ends and the other starts.

The Harry Potter Alliance's campaign against Wal-Mart offers us one vivid example of what this cultural practice might look like. The HP Alliance[1] encouraged a generation of young people who learned to read and write from the *Harry Potter* books to also use J. K. Rowling's world as a platform for civic engagement. The *Harry Potter* series depicted its youth protagonists questioning adult authority, fighting evil, and standing up for their rights. The HP Alliance has launched a series of online campaigns which merge fan cultural production with activist politics. During one such campaign, the HP Alliance partnered with Wal-Mart Watch, a group backed by the Service Employees International Union as a focal point for criticism for the retail chain's employment practices. The HP Alliance and the Boston-based comedy troupe The Late Night Players translated the union's agenda into a series of campy, over-the-top videos depicting further adventures impacting Hogwarts and the wizarding world. Harry and Hermoine (who is played in drag) discover that the traditional business in Diagon Alley have been closed by 'you know which superstore' and must do battle with Lord Waldemart (whose sinister practices include exploiting his house elves, driving out local competitors, and refusing to provide health care to his underlings). The YouTube circulation of these spoofs,[2] in turn, drove traffic back to the Wal-Mart Watch website, where one could find a more straightforward discussion of their cause.

Jonathan Zittrain (2008) has argued that certain technologies are 'generative' in that they encourage users to tinker with them and adapt them to their own needs. The result is user-led innovation. Yet, what makes YouTube 'generative' in Zittrain's sense has little to do with its technological structures (which arguably support individual rather than collaborative effort) and has everything to do with the ways YouTube has been adopted by various participatory cultures. I've argued elsewhere (Jenkins *et al.*, 2006) that a participatory culture is one which not only lowers the barriers to participation but also creates strong social incentives to produce and share what one produces with others. Arguably, many people are taking advantage of the distribution platform YouTube provides, in part, because they feel the emotional support of a community eager to see their productions.

Benkler (2006) offers a second argument for why a space like YouTube might be 'generative': 'These practices make their practitioners better 'readers' of their own culture and more self-reflective and critical of the culture they occupy, thereby enabling them to become more self-reflective participants in conversations within that culture' (Benkler, 2006: 15). Even if many of them have not yet chosen to participate, they understand their place in the media ecology differently because they know how easy it is to contribute content. In short, YouTube as a platform, participatory culture as an ethos inspires a new kind of subjectivity which transforms all consumers into potential authors.

You Can't Stop the Signal

From the start, YouTube represented a challenge to the 'stickiness' model which has long determined the value of Internet culture: it is not a 'roach motel' which grabs and holds onto consumers by locking down content. Rather, the YouTube business model creates value through circulation. Its distinctive technical affordances makes porting YouTube content elsewhere a trivial matter of copying and pasting code, allowing videos to be inserted into diverse cultural economies and social ecologies. Yet, this uncontrolled flow of media content creates ambivalences and anxieties – not simply for commercial rights holders but also among amateur media makers. Consider, for example, the case of fan music vids, which remix footage from cult television programs to popular music, creating a distinctive form of cultural commentary. While much remix culture takes the form of parody, this genre intensifies the emotional experience of the original, taking us deeper into the thoughts and feelings of central characters.

When a recent news story traced fan videos back to 'the dawn of YouTube,' many female fans expressed outrage. For more than two decades, a community, composed mostly of women, had been producing such videos, using two VCRs and patch cords, struggling with roll back and rainbow lines, when it seemed an act of sisyphean patience. Francesca Coppa (2007) traces the history of this form back to 1975 when a woman named Kandy Fong first put together slide show presentations set to popular songs for *Star Trek* conventions. Over the years, these fan vidders developed more sophisticated techniques as they embraced and mastered digital editing tools, constructed their own distribution channels, and defined and refined multiple aesthetic traditions.

Yet, even as other 'remix' communities found a supportive home on YouTube, the community struggled with how public they wanted to make their practices. When I wrote *Textual Poachers* in 1992, the vidders were reluctant to talk and most asked not to be named. Fans were nervous that their works were vulnerable to prosecution for copyright violation from film studios, networks, and recording studios alike. They were also anxious that their videos would not be understood outside of the interpretive context fandom provided. For example, when a Kirk/Spock vid, set to Nine Inch Nails's 'Closer,' leaked onto YouTube without its creator's permission, its queer reading of the *Star Trek* characters as lovers was widely read as comic, even though this particular work was seen as disturbing within the slash fan community because of its vivid depiction of sexual violence (Jenkins, 2007).

Some vidders circulated their works through less visible channels, such as IMeem,[3] often friend-locked so that they could only be accessed within their own close-knit community. Debates broke out on LiveJournal and at fan conventions as veteran vidders were torn between a fear of being written out of the history of mashup culture and an anxiety about what would happen if the Powers That Be (producers and networks) learned what they were doing. In Fall 2007, *New York* magazine ran a profile of Luminosity, a leader in the viding movement (Hill, 2007), while fan vids were showcased, alongside the work of other subcultural communities, at a DIY Media conference hosted by University of Southern California.

As Laura Shapiro (2006), a contributor to the USC event, explained in a Live Journal post:

> However legitimate a vidder's fears may be, the fact is that the vids are already out there. The minute we put our vids online, we expose ourselves to the world . . . We can't stop people from sharing our vids without our consent or even our knowledge. We can't control the distribution of our own work in a viral medium . . . We also can't control other people's attitudes. New vidders arrive on the scene every day, without any historical context or legal fears, and plunk their vids onto YouTube without a second thought. They post publicly and promote themselves enthusiastically, and why not? That's what everybody does on the Internet, from the AMV creators to machinima-makers to *Brokeback Mountain* parodists to political remixers.

Shapiro's post to the Live Journal viding community suggests the complex creative, personal, institutional, ideological, and legal motivations which might draw such a historically sheltered subculture toward greater public outreach:

- recognition of our history and traditions, academically and socially (new vidders learn, older vidders are venerated)
- the opportunity to provide context and normalize our fannish work the way traditionally male fannish work is becoming normalized
- the potential for vidders to connect fannish work with professional work, working professionally in the entertainment industry if they want to

- more widespread appreciation and recognition of great vids and great vidders
- the potential to generate widespread support for us in any legal battles we may encounter (joining forces with other DIY video communities, representation of the Electronic Frontiers Foundation, creation of legal defense funds, etc.)
- the potential for cross-pollination or even unification of disparate vidding communities and the chance to connect isolated vidders with those communities
- the chance to influence Big Media to create more of the kinds of TV shows and movies we value
- the potential to influence the wider viewing world with themes and portrayals of sexual and gender equality, homosexuality, etc.

There is nothing inevitable about YouTube's current status as *the* platform for circulating user-generated content. News coverage assumes, 'If we build it, they will come,' when in fact, many groups struggle with whether 'To YouTube or Not to YouTube.' There are certainly reasons to seek broader public circulation of their materials – especially in the case of media makers who wanted to gain access to the media industry – but not every amateur media maker wants to turn pro. There certainly are reasons to want to circulate messages beyond one's own community – especially in the case of various kinds of media activists – but not every amateur media maker wants to change the world. Fame may be the name of the game for some but not for all.

The Gift Economy Meets Commodity Culture

The female fans in the viding community, for example, have argued that their creative efforts reflect the logic of a gift economy where goods are circulated freely for shared benefit rather than sold for profit. In his book, *The Gift: Imagination and the Erotic Life of Property*, Lewis Hyde (2007: xxi) argues that a gift economy is shaped by 'the obligation to give, the obligation to accept, and the obligation to reciprocate,' rather than by financial incentives. Hyde (2007: xx) writes,

> Unlike the sale of a commodity, the giving of a gift tends to establish a relationship between the parties involved. Furthermore, when gifts circulate within a group, their commerce leaves a series of interconnected relationships in its wake, and a kind of decentralized cohesiveness emerges.

Hyde's account consistently contrasts the economic value that motivates a commodity culture with the alternative senses of worth ('status,' 'prestige,' or 'esteem') that shape the exchange of gifts (Hyde, 2007: 104). YouTube seeks to transform the free exchange of cultural 'gifts' into an attention economy monetized through advertising revenue.

Increasingly, voices in the fan community argue against this commodity logic as threatening the social relationships that have grown up around their production activities. Instead, they push for the creation of nonprofit channels[4] to enable them freely to share their productions. They are not eager to see others make money off of their creative labor but that doesn't necessarily mean they are ready to turn their passionate expressions into work for hire. Some fans have embraced 'The Geek Manifesto' (The Geek Community, 2008) as an expression of their opposition to the imposition of mainstream or commercial values upon the alternative culture they have constructed:

> This is ours. It will always be ours. You will never grok it, unless you become one of us. Do not try to make it yours. Do not try to co-opt it for your own ends. If it inspires you to create your own thing, then fine. The thing that you create though is not the thing we have created. Do not pretend otherwise.

One such effort to re-assert control over their own cultural practices is the Organization for Transformative Works. The OTW asserted as its mission:[5] 'to work toward a future in which all fannish works are recognized as legal and transformative, and accepted as legitimate creative activity.' The group is working not only to create alternative, noncommercial sites for content distribution but also to organize legal and intellectual defenses of their traditional practices.

The Case of Activist Video

Fans are not the only group concerned about what happens when amateur media content is removed from its original reception and production contexts. Inspired by the public outcry surrounding the home video footage of the beating of Rodney King by the Los Angeles police in the 1980s, musician Peter Gabriel launched the human rights organization, Witness, as a way of expanding access to video production technology so that oppressed people world-wide could speak back to power. As Witness activist Sam Gregory (Jenkins, 2008b) explains, shifts in the technical infrastructure, including the emergence of YouTube, have dramatically expanded the organization's capacity to respond to human rights abuses:

> Our work has also always blurred the line between amateurs and professionals in terms of using video – we are training human rights workers, and now concerned citizens, to use video as an everyday facet of their work, rather than to turn them into docu-mentary film-makers . . . We've seen a progressive expansion of the participatory possibilities of video: first, increased access to cameras, the increased access to editing capacity, then the dra-matic growth of online video-sharing for distribution. And in the past three years we see the possibilities for increased collabora-tion in editing and production, for online distribution, and for more immediate and widespread filming – all facilitated by a digitally literate youth, by mobile technology with still image and video capability and by new online tools.

Gregory (in Jenkins, 2008b) recognizes the value of what YouTube offers:

> From an advocacy perspective, we can see how IF a video achieves either prominent placement, or takes off virally on YouTube it can take off in terms of public prominence. Similarly for many non-governmental advocacy organizations that are trying to engage a general public either with a single video or via a channel, YouTube is likely to be the first place that public will look. And we also recognize

that YouTube is a pushing-out point for footage that finds homes in many other subculture-specific media systems, including human rights, where it is embedded and re-contextualized.

Yet, like Shapiro and the fan vidders, Gregory is concerned that his videos often get decontextualized as they enter this hybrid media space:

As human rights video circulates increasingly unmoored from its original location – i.e. embedded, shared, remixed – it becomes key to place context and ways to act within the video and imagery itself rather than outside it since no sooner has your video been forwarded from YouTube . . . it becomes de-coupled from options to act unless those are built into the video itself, and unless your message comes through loud and clear.

As a consequence, the organization has chosen to construct its own site, The Hub, to support the sharing of human rights videos with already committed activists, even as it continues to circulate at least some materials through YouTube.

In some cases, this potential to decontextualize and recontextualize video content has a progressive potential. Gregory notes, for example, that some of the most effective videos for directing public consciousness against human rights violations were produced not by victims but by perpetrators, who originally deployed the videos as a means of intimidation and public humilation or who were simply indifferent to the ways their actions might be perceived stripped of their justifying discourses. Yet, the same thing might happen in reverse should viewers take pleasure or remain indifferent to the human suffering depicted in human rights videos, unable to separate their graphic imagery from YouTube's entertainment content.

In a hybrid space like YouTube, it is often very difficult to determine what regimes of truth govern different genres of user-generated content. The goals of communicators can no longer be simply read off the channels of communication. Witness the emergence of Astroturf – fake grassroots media-content produced by commercial media companies and special interest groups but passed off as coming from individual amateurs. Historically, these powerful interests could exert overt control over broadcast media but now, they often have to mask their power in order to operate within network culture. *Al Gore's Penguin Army*[6] is perhaps the best-known example of Astroturf. This cut-up animation spoof of *An Inconvenient Truth* was first posted by a user named Toutsmith from Beverley Hills but further investigation revealed that it was professionally produced by the DCI Group, a commercial advertising firm whose clients included General Motors and ExxonMobil; the firm also had historically produced content for the Republican Party. Or consider the uncertainties surrounding the notorious Lonelygirl15, a story recounted in greater detail earlier in this book. She initially presented her confessional videos as an 'authentic' videoblog, later claimed them to be an 'art project' before they were finally discovered to be connected to a commercial media company. Yet, it's worth remembering that we know about these examples of 'Astroturf' because the YouTube public was suspicious of these materials and worked collectively to trace their roots.

Before we dismiss this all as 'postmodern,' keep in mind the elaborate play between reality and fiction set in motion in the nineteenth century, which writer Neil Harris (1973) has described as the golden age of the 'humbug.' Harris writes about the proliferation of fake 'mermaids' and stone giants at a time when knowledge was in flux, science was at least partially amateur and participatory, new discoveries (both anthropological and technological) were being made every day, and people wanted to acquire new skills at discernment to keep up with the pace of cultural churn. The circulation and debunking of such hoaxes facilitated 'a form of intellectual exercise, simulating even when literal truth could not be determined' (Harris, 1973: 75). In other words, there seems to be a fascination with blurry categories at moments of media in transition – it is one of the ways we apply our evolving skills in a context where the categories that organize our culture are in flux. Some groups can tap this fascination with blurred ontological categories as an end unto itself, as is certainly the case with alternative reality games which typically never acknowledge their status as games. Other groups, such as Witness, demand that we understand the realities their videos depict.

Plenitude and Diversity

YouTube's utopian possibilities must be read against the dysto-pian realities of a world where people have uneven access to the means of participation and where many are discouraged from even trying. If YouTube creates value around amateur content, it doesn't distribute value equally. Some forms of cultural production are embraced within the mainstream tastes of site visitors and the commercial interests of the site owners. Other forms of cultural production are pushed to the margins as falling outside dominant tastes and interests. And some – amateur porn, nudist videos, etc. – are excluded altogether. The impact of such exclusions and mar-ginalizations were apparent to John McMurria (2006):

> A glance at the top 100 rated, viewed and disused videos, and most subscribed channels reveals far less racial diversity than broadcast network television . . . Perhaps we might think about the difference between what it means to be a YouTube commu-nity and what it would take to use the YouTube video sharing technologies to help expand the movement for racial and eco-nomic justice.

McMurria's critique of YouTube suggests that a participatory cul-ture is not necessarily a diverse culture. Leave aside inequalities in terms of access to technology or educational training needed to become fully engaged in YouTube, leave aside the number of users who can access the web only through public terminals which do not support the posting of video, there is the majori-tarian logic built into current mechanisms of user-moderation. YouTube pushes up content which receives support from other users. While such mechanisms seem democratic, they have the effect of hiding minority perspectives. Minority content certainly circulates on YouTube, traveling through a range of social net-works to reach niche publics, but there's little or no chance that such content will reach a larger viewership because of the scale on which YouTube operates. How many visitors to the site move below the most visible content, especially if they don't already have a stake in the topics or the communities involved?

Writing in the *Chronicle of Higher Education* (19 May 2006), Bill Ivey, the former chairman of the National Endowment for the Arts, and Steven J. Tepper, a professor of Sociology at Vanderbilt University, described what they see as the long-term consequences of this participation gap:

> Increasingly, those who have the education, skills, financial resources, and time required to navigate the sea of cultural choice will gain access to new cultural opportunities . . . They will be the pro-ams who network with other serious amateurs and find audiences for their work. They will discover new forms of cultural expression that engage their passions and help them forge their own identities, and will be the curators of their own expressive lives and the mavens who enrich the lives of others . . . At the same time, those citizens who have fewer resources – less time, less money, and less knowledge about how to navigate the cultural system – will increasingly rely on the cultural fare offered to them by consolidated media and entertainment conglomerates . . . Such citizens will be trapped on the wrong side of the cultural divide. So technology and economic change are conspiring to create a new cultural elite – and a new cultural underclass . . . Can America prosper if its citizens experience such different and unequal cultural lives? (Ivey and Tepper, 2006: B6)

YouTube seems to offer an inexhaustible supply of user-generated content. Yet, this very plentitude (McCracken, 1998) may discourage us from pondering what materials are not to be found there. The DIY movement historically sought to get production equipment into the hands of groups who are under-represented in the commercial mainstream so that they can get their stories out and have their voices heard. If we see YouTube as operating without a history, we erase the politics behind those struggles and we may end up accepting far less than what we have bargained for. By reclaiming what happened before YouTube, we may have a basis for judging how well YouTube really is serving the cause of participatory culture and we may find openings for 'a critique, a goal, a community, and a context' of the kind that motivated earlier DIY media makers.

Uses of YouTube: Digital Literacy and the Growth of Knowledge

John Hartley

YIRNing for YouTube

I invented YouTube. Well, not YouTube exactly, but something close – something called YIRN; and not by myself exactly, but with a team. In 2003–5 I led a research project designed to link geographically dispersed young people, to allow them to post their own photos, videos and music, and to comment on the same from various points of view – peer to peer, author to public, or impresario to audience. We wanted to find a way to take the individual creative productivity that is associated with the Internet and combine it with the easy accessibility and openness to other people's imagination that is associated with broadcasting; especially, in the context of young people, listening to the radio. So we called it the Youth Internet Radio Network, or YIRN.[1]

As researchers, we wanted to understand how young people interact as both consumers and producers of new media content, especially of material made by their peers. We were also interested in the interface between non-market self-expression and commercial creative content (where music has always been exemplary). We wanted to trace the process by means of which individual creative talent may lead to economic enterprise and employment; and in general to understand how culture and creativity may be a seedbed for innovation and enterprise.

In order to find out the answers to our research questions, we thought we would need to set up the appropriate website for young people to 'stick their stuff,' which we would then observe by means of 'ethnographic action research' (Tacchi, Hearn, and Ninan 2004), and if all went well we would make a contribution to rural and remote skills-development and regional sustainability. In the event the workshops we held to train young people in techniques like digital storytelling did go well, but we spent two years failing to get the web interface right. Eventually we developed a site called '*Sticky.net*' ('a place to stick your stuff'), but by the time we'd fixed the functionality and solved technical, design, security and IP issues the project was over, the kids had moved on, and the site was barely populated. We had invented the idea of YouTube but failed to get it right in practice and in time, possibly because we were more interested in our research questions than in monetizing consumer creativity. Well, that's what we told each other. Certainly it would have helped to be in the midst of mental California when the zeitgeist, the kids, and the technology happened to overlap. But we simply weren't.

YIRN was productive in the way that failure can be – it spawned quite a few bigger-and-better research projects in urban informatics, digital storytelling, youth creative enterprise, and development communication, even if it didn't succeed in establishing a robust network for Queensland's creative youth. Later, as bandwidth finally expanded sufficiently to allow the Internet to shift from text and music to video, YouTube 'proper' came along, with its simple slogan 'Broadcast Yourself,' its easy useability (Flash), and its willingness to scale straight up, in no time flat, from 'me' (the first video being 'Me at the Zoo' by co-founder Jawed Karim) to 'global.' It was clear that neither Queensland youth nor anyone else needed their own special playground; much better to be part of a global commons where you might meet anyone. This is what YouTube quickly provided, and it taught me some lessons straight away: that the open network is more important than anything else; that success comes from being in the right place at the right time; and that simplicity, ease of use and accessibility are more important than functionality, control, or purposive direction.

Just as our funding ran out, YouTube was launched. Unlike us, it took off without displaying much interest in what the broadcast-yourself generation might want to use this newfound capability *for*; how it might be shaped toward imaginative, instrumental, or intellectual ends. It simply . . . evolved.

But however successful YouTube has become, its evolution has left some questions unanswered. What do people need (to have, to know, to do) in order to participate in YouTube? Also, what results from just leaving it alone and letting learning happen by evolutionary random copying or contagion, rather than by 'disciplined' teaching? And what might be expected if 'we' – the users – decided to make a platform like YouTube useful not just for self-expression and communication but for description and argumentation too – for 'objective' as well as 'subjective' knowledge, in Karl Popper's terms (Popper, 1972: ch. 3)?

When we set up YIRN we assumed that we needed to be active in the field of 'digital literacy.' We thought you had to start by teaching users to make and upload content, and that you couldn't just leave them to their own devices as YouTube does. The downside of the YouTube model (of learning by doing and random copying) is that people don't necessarily learn what they need to express what they want. The upside is that very often they learn from each other, in the process of expanding the archive, and their efforts in turn teach others – just like YouTube celebrities 'Geriatric 1927' (Peter Oakley) or 'Tasha & Dishka' (Lital Mizel and Adi Frimmerman) of 'Hey Clip' fame. From this, more questions arise, about different models of education:

- Do new media of communication like YouTube and other Internet affordances (open source programming, wikis, blogging, social networks, social bookmark folksonomies and the rest) require investment (public or private) in teaching whole populations how to use them? Or do they do better by blind experimentation and adaptation?
- Does the investment in the existing infrastructure of formal education have anything to offer? But if schools, colleges, and universities are not the right vehicle, why not, and what is?
- Can we imagine a hybrid formal/informal (expert/amateur; public/private) mode of propagation for learning 'digital literacy,' and if so how might YouTube play a part?

- How might YouTube be exploited for scientific, journalistic, and imaginative purposes as well as for self-expression, communication, and file-sharing?

Print to Digital Literacy

One way to address such questions is to compare digital literacy with its predecessor – print literacy. The nineteenth and twentieth centuries were notable for massive and sustained public investment in schools and (later on) universities – the infrastructure needed to deliver near-universal print-literacy at low cost to the user. Right around the world the enormous cost was justified in order to produce modern citizens and a disciplined, skilled workforce for industrialization. That effort has not been matched in the digital era. The physical ICT infrastructure that has developed since the 1990s for organizational, residential, and lately mobile connectivity has not been matched by a concomitant investment in education – public or private – to promote its creative uptake and use by entire populations. Usage across different demographics is patchy to say the least, continuing to reproduce the class and demographic divides inherited from the industrial era. The scaling up of digital literacy is left largely to entertainment providers seeking eyeballs for advertisers, and those who want consumers for their proprietary software applications; in other words, to the market.

If we are to believe what we read about Generation Y and 'digital natives,' they are already in evolutionary mid-step. Today's high-school entrants – those who'll be retiring from work around the year 2060 – seem almost a different species from modernists reared in the image of industry. Teens evidently don't see computers as technology. It's as if they have developed an innate ability for text-messaging, iPodding, gaming, and multitasking on multiple platforms. They can share their life story on Facebook, entertain each other on YouTube, muse philosophically in the blogosphere, contribute to knowledge on Wikipedia, create cutting-edge art on Flickr, and compile archives on Del.icio.us. Some can do most of these things at once, and then submit their efforts to an online ethic of collective intelligence and iterative improvability that is surely scientific in mode.

But they learn very little of this in school. For the most part the education system has responded to the digital era by prohibiting school-based access to digital environments including YouTube, apart from 'walled gardens' under strict teacher control.[2] From this, kids also learn that formal education's top priority is not to make them digitally literate but to 'protect' them from 'inappropriate' content and online predators. So a good many of them switch off, and devote their energies to daydreaming and making mischief. And there's the rub. *Daydreaming* is just another word for *identity-formation* using individual imagination. *Mischief* is no more than *experimental engagement* with peer-groups and places. Teenage daydreaming (self-expression) and mischief (communication) have been the wellspring of the entertainment industry from time immemorial, supplying the characters, actions, plots, and lyrics of fantasy fiction from *A Midsummer Night's Dream* to *I Know What You Did Last Summer*. Popular culture has prospered by capturing the attention, mood, time, activities, and culture of young people (and others) in their leisure moments, when they're just beyond the institutional grasp of family, school, or work. So while schools and universities keep their distance, *purposeless entertainment* has nurtured demand for creative self-expression and communication among the young.

Until recently, that demand has been provided on a take-it-or-leave-it basis by experts and corporations with little input (apart from cash) by the consumers themselves. But now, with digital online media, there's almost infinite scope for DIY (do-it-yourself) and DIWO (do-it-with-others) creative content produced by and for consumers and users, without the need for institutional filtering or control bureaucracies. The so-called 'long tail' of self-made content is accessible to anyone near a computer terminal. Everyone is a potential publisher. Instead of needing to rely on the expertise of others, young people navigate themselves through this universe of information. Although schools and universities certainly teach 'ICT skills' and even 'creative practice,' so far they have not proven to be adept at enabling demand-driven and distributed learning networks for imaginative rather than instrumental purposes. They continue to push the literate modern technologies of *library* and *laboratory* – as if these hold a monopoly on knowledge – because they cannot figure out the complexities of the open system *labyrinth*.

Despite the democratizing energies of advocates for literacy, and despite universal schooling, print-literate culture has resulted in a de facto division of labor between those who use print as an autonomous means of communication and those who use it – if at all – for private consumption. While most people can read, in print very few *publish*. Hence active contribution to science, journalism and even fictional storytelling tends to be restricted to expert elites, while most of the population makes do with limited and commercialized 'uses of literacy,' as Richard Hoggart pointed out half a century ago (1957).

But the Internet does not distinguish between literacy and publication. So now it is possible to imagine population-wide literacy in which everyone has the ability to contribute as well as consume. They can certainly use the Internet for daydreaming and mischief – self-expression and communication – but it is quite possible to move on to other levels of functionality, and other purposes, including science, journalism and works of the imagination like the novel, those great inventions of print literacy, which must be transformed in the process. Despite misgivings among those with something to lose, these great realist textual systems don't have to be confined to authorized elites any more.

Updating TV's 'Bardic Function'

Recently both business strategies and public-service thinking have stressed the need for organizations, governments, and communities to evolve models of innovation that go beyond the closed expert process of the literate-industrial era. In a knowledge society, what's needed instead is an open innovation network. At the same time, the intuitive and imaginative skills of entrepreneurs in pursuit of 'creative destruction' and renewal can be compared with those of artists. The need for creativity in all aspects of economic and political life has been recognized. Creative talent commands economic as well as symbolic value. But an open innovation network benefits from harnessing the creative energies of the whole population, not just the inputs of isolated expert elites. With technologically enabled social networks using digital media, productivity can now be expected from consumers as well as producers, as users extend the growth of knowledge far beyond what can be achieved by professionals publishing in print. Hence, YouTube (among other online social networking sites), with all its unsystematic exuberance and unambitious content, devoted to no more than mucking around or, as the classic 'Hey clip'[3] puts it, 'heya all! dancing stupid is fun,' is *simultaneously* the complex system in which digital literacy can find new purposes, new publishers, and new knowledge. And anyone can join in, which ups the productivity of the whole system.

Thus far the commercial media and entertainment industries have pursued an industrial or expert-system model of production, where professionals manufacture stories, experiences and identities for the rest of us to consume. This system is 'representative,' both in the sense that 'we' are represented onscreen and in the sense that a tiny band of professionals 'represents' us all. The productivity of this system is measured not by the number of ideas propagated or stories told, but by the number of dollars earned per story. Thus, over the past century, cinema, radio, and television have all organized and scaled human storytelling into an industrial system, where millions watch but mere hundreds do the writing. Broadcast media speak to and on behalf of us all in mass anonymous cultures.

This is what I once called the 'bardic function' (Fiske and Hartley 2003; see also Hartley 2008c). Now that we can 'do it ourselves' – and 'do it with others' too – what might become of television's 'bardic function'? YouTube is the first large-scale answer to that question. Its slogan 'Broadcast yourself' neatly captures the difference between old-style TV and new. YouTube massively scales up both the number of people *publishing* TV 'content' and the number of videos available to be watched. However, few of the videos are 'stories' as traditionally understood, not least because of radically reduced timeframes: ninety minutes for cinema; thirty to fifty minutes for TV, and one to two minutes for most YouTube. The best stories, for instance *Lonleygirl15*, pretend to be something else in order to conform to the conventions of dialogic social networks.[4]

YouTube allows everyone to perform their own 'bardic function.' Just grab a harp (even an 'air harp') and sing![5] With other social network enterprises, both commercial and community-based, it is a practical experiment in what a 'bottom-up' (all-singing, all-dancing) model of a 'bardic' system might look like in a technologically enabled culture. Instead of looking for a *social institution* or an *economic sector* like the original Celtic bardic order or the television industry, both characterized by expertise, restricted access, control, regulation, and one-way communication, it is now possible to look for an *enabling social technology*, with near-ubiquitous and near-universal access, where individual agents can navigate large-scale networks for their own purposes, while simultaneously contributing to the growth of knowledge and the archive of the possible. The Internet has rapidly evolved into a new 'enabling social technology' *for knowledge*. And just as 'new' media typically supplement rather than supplant their predecessors, it relies on both experts and everyone. It is the means by which 'bottom-up' (DIY consumer-based) and 'top-down' (industrial expert-based) knowledge-generation connects and interacts (Potts *et al.*, 2008a; Hartley 2009).

YouTube is Semiospherical

Human language is the primary model for this dynamic process of individuated productivity and action within an open complex system. Language, in general and in each distinct language, is only ever produced by individuals, but it expresses and connects a community as large in principle as all those who speak it, including the ones not yet alive who can read it later on, at least until it changes beyond recognition. A language is a network, but one of a special kind: what Albert-László Barabási (2002) has identified as a 'scale-free network':

> The brain is a network of nerve cells connected by axons, and cells themselves are networks of molecules connected by biochemical reactions. Societies, too, are networks of people linked by friendships, familial relationships and professional ties. On a larger scale, food webs and ecosystems can be represented as networks of species. And networks pervade technology: the Internet, power grids and transportation systems are but a few examples. Even the language we are using to convey these thoughts to you is a network, made up of words connected by syntactic relationships. (Barabási and Bonabeau, 2003: 50)

Barabási and Bonabeau (2003: 50) explain that scale-free networks are characterized by many 'nodes' with a few links to others in the network, and a few 'hubs' with many links to other nodes. Complex networks appear to be organized by 'fundamental laws' that apply across to the physical, social and communicative worlds:

> Such discoveries have dramatically changed what we thought we knew about the complex interconnected world around us. Unexplained by previous network theories, hubs offer convincing proof that various complex systems have a strict architecture, ruled by fundamental laws that appear to apply equally to cells, computers, languages and society.

Such insights can begin to explain how myriad individual points of origin and action are nevertheless linked into a coherent system, in which order emerges spontaneously and without the need for overall centralized control (Shirky 2008). Like language, the human network is itself networked, branched, and differentiated. It can be understood both (anthropologically, structurally) as whole, and (romantically, culturally) in its particulars.

The characteristics of complex adaptive systems apply to markets as well as to languages. Scale-free networks are characterized by *growth* (addition of new nodes), *preferential attachment* (new nodes seek links with already linked hubs), and *hierarchical clustering*, where 'small, tightly interlinked clusters of nodes are connected into larger, less cohesive groups' (Barabási and Bonabeau, 2003: 58).[6] It took the emergence of computational power to be able to model this kind of system mathematically, but that is now under way, in the economic sphere as well as in the 'enabling' sciences – particularly in evolutionary and complexity economics (Beinhocker, 2006). Here the concept of 'preferential attachment' explains the principle of social network markets, whose special characteristic is that agents' choices (agents being both consumers and producers, both individuals and enterprises) are *determined by the choices of others* in the network (Ormerod, 2001; Potts *et al.*, 2008a). Being able to see systems as whole and in terms of individual agency also has the effect, by the way, of reuniting the long-divergent 'two paradigms' of structuralism (system; whole) and culturalism (agency; particular) that have driven cultural studies since Raymond Williams (Hall, 1980).

The models that the network and scientists are coming up with look like language-models: a system in which nodes (agents/speakers) and relationships (links/communication) interconnect in an open complex network, coordinated by relatively few major hubs or 'institutions of language' including media organizations. This is Yuri Lotman's (1990) 'universe of the mind' – the 'semiosphere' – another name for which is culture. When modelled mathematically, culture emerges not in *structured opposition* to economics (as cultural critics hold) but as part of the same *coordinated network*. YouTube is one such network.

A Message from the Ancients

Much of human storytelling is 'said and done.' It is over with as soon as uttered, because most stories – most utterances – are part of what the linguist Roman Jakobson called *phatic* communication, checking the connection between speakers not creating new knowledge. So most stories are ephemera not archive. This function may predominate, along with emotive (self-expression)

and conative (imperative) language use, among small tightly connected clusters such as families and friends, in which each agent
or node has few links and the message is uttered to maintain
those links (which is why phatic communication is often called
'grooming talk'). This is why the Internet has a lot of small-talk
and chat and much less Shakespeare and science.

But some stories are not mere phatic exchange. Their function
is not to connect the speakers but to describe the world or crea-
tively to expand the system's capabilities. In Jakobson's (1958)
terms (see also Fiske and Hartley, 2003: 62–3), their function is
not phatic but *referential* (information about the context), *poetic*
(self-referential), or *metalinguistic* (about the code or system).
Such stories may cumulatively become 'hubbed,' with myriad
links radiating across the network, playing a coordinating role.
They might be myths, urban and otherwise, folklore or 'tales of
yore'; or they might be retold in highly elaborated form, as song,
drama or narrative. The point is that they retain myriad points of
origin (being retold afresh by all and sundry), but also recogniz-
able shape and coherence.

Writing about modern art in the context of the 'theatricality of
ordinary behavior,' Göran Sonesson (2002) argues that with the
abolition of the modernist distinction between fine and popular
arts in postmodernity, it is possible to see that fine arts borrow
something new from popular arts, which themselves borrow it
from ordinary life, namely the *phatic* function *as art*.

> Contemporary arts . . . repeat everyday, trivial situations, which
> have become standardized and repeatable, not because of the
> presence of some popular memory, but because of being pro-
> jected over and over again by television and other mass-media:
> they exist thanks to the *bardic* function of television, as Fiske &
> Hartley call it, that is, in Jakobson's terms, thanks to the phatic
> function. (Sonesson, 2002: 24)

The argument here is that all three spheres of ordinary life, popular media, and fine art are fully interconnected in a larger cultural
network, and that art itself has reached the stage of development
where it can recognize and gain inspiration from the most basic

or banal functions of language. Although there's a lot of negative evaluation in public commentary on these matters, with banality, media, art, and postmodernism all coming in for a good tongue-lashing, some important insights have been 'discovered' in this process: namely, that the *performance of the self* is just as coded, 'theatrical' and 'artistic' in ordinary life as it is in fine art; that subjectivity links power and aesthetics in performance; and that there is an open channel of mutual influence among these different hierarchical levels of the overall cultural network (manifested for instance in 'gossip' media and celebrity culture, where the attention accorded to celebrities like Paris and Britney is focused on their personal lives, which for others constitute the condition of ordinariness).

As a result, it is possible to re-evaluate phatic communication itself. This is necessary in the context of digital media like YouTube, since so much of what is published in social network sites is phatic. To the modernist eye, trained in literate expertise, which seeks to minimize phatic utterances, it looks a proper mess. However, the problem here may be in the eye of the critical-literate beholder, not in the uses of the Internet, for a medium in which phatic communication can be restored to full performative theatricality may also be restoring an ancient, multi-voiced mode of narration to cultural visibility. For example Anil Dash, VP of Six Apart Ltd and early adopter of blogging, has argued that:

> TV and newspapers and radio and books, especially in the West in the last 100 years, have dwindled down from a stream of thousands of concurrent parallel conversations to the serial streaming of the Big Six or Seven media companies. The train-of-thought, rambling, narrative tradition of human interaction which dates back to the earliest storytelling traditions of our species has been abandoned for bullet points. (Dash, 1999)

The implication of Dash's argument is that the web opens up 'public discourse' in a way that enhances ancient competences, which are distributed across the species, not restricted to the 'Big Six or Seven.' He argues that asides, interjections by third parties, annotation, hyperlinks and so on, all of which character-ize YouTube, add to the credibility, richness and critical value of a web-published document, which emerges not as a linear per-formance of the authorial self but as a concurrent performance of connectedness, collective intelligence, and oral modes of sto-rytelling. If this is so, then it is important to understand better the 'train-of-thought, rambling, narrative tradition of human interaction,' because instead of dismissing it as phatic inconse-quentiality, bad art or non-science it may be time to reappraise it as an intellectual resource. If storytelling – not to mention rambling – is an ancient resource, it may be wise to abandon invidious distinctions between different media, and to see them as part of the growth of knowledge, going back to the 'earliest storytelling traditions of our species.' The cultural ubiquity of a restricted number of story-types, coming down from time imme-morial, has led some to conclude that there is very little variety among plots. Joseph Campbell was a proponent of this view, proposing that a 'monomyth' runs as follows:

> A hero ventures forth from the world of common day into a region of supernatural wonder: fabulous forces are there encountered and a decisive victory is won: the hero comes back from this mys-terious adventure with the power to bestow boons on his fellow man. (Campbell, 1949: 30)

The 'structural' analysis of myth and folklore also preoccupied the structuralists and formalists – Propp, Greimas, Todorov, Lotman, and Bettelheim (Hawkes, 1977).

More recently, Christopher Booker (2004) has identified seven basic plots that are structural transformations of ancient tales:

1. Overcoming the Monster
2. Rags to Riches
3. The Quest
4. Voyage and Return
5. Rebirth
6. Comedy
7. Tragedy

The most basic plot, 'overcoming the monster,' which character-izes the oldest surviving story in the world, the *Epic of Gilgamesh*, is also present in the classical stories of Perseus and Theseus, the Anglo-Saxon poem *Beowulf*, 'fairytales' like Little Red Riding Hood, Dracula, and in contemporary times H. G. Wells' *War of the Worlds*, or movies like *Seven Samurai*, *Dr No*, *Star Wars: A New Hope*, *Jaws* – and the 2007 3D-movie/anime hybrid *Beowulf*.

This kind of story is used to structure truth as well as fiction, news and politics as well as movies, and in exactly the same way. Such narratives are part of what Robin Andersen (2006) has called 'militainment.' A good example would be the news coverage of George W. Bush's 'Mission accomplished' speech on board the *USS Abraham Lincoln* (1 May 2003), declaring both decisive victory in Iraq over 'a great evil' – an unseen monster worthy of *Beowulf*'s Grendel – and spelling out the boons bestowed by the heroes. Naturally the event has been clipped, spoofed and re-versioned on YouTube.[7] The final paragraph of the President's speech explicitly ties the events of the day to 'a message that is ancient':

> All of you – all in this generation of our military – have taken up the highest calling of history. You are defending your country, and protecting the innocent from harm. And wher-ever you go, you carry a message of hope – a message that is ancient, and ever new. In the words of the prophet Isaiah: 'To the captives, "Come out!" and to those in darkness, "Be free!"'[8]

Of course this story came back to haunt the Bush administration, but not because of its status as myth; only because the monster wasn't dead. It wasn't a *good* story.

'Those Who Tell Stories Rule Society' – Narrative Science

Booker's own method for discerning pattern in repetition was to read a lot of stories, and to explain the patterns in terms of Jungian archetypes, which he uses to link stories to the process of individual 'self-realization.' He also suggested that the science he was trying to found was long overdue:

> One day, I believe, it will eventually be seen that for a long time one of the most remarkable failures of our scientific approach to understanding the world was not to perceive that our urge to imagine stories is something just as much governed by laws which lay it open to scientific investigation as the structures of the atom or the genome. (Booker, 2004: 700)

Reviewers were impressed with the laws; less so with the enabling theory. Denis Dutton (2005), for instance:[9]

> The basic situations of fiction are a product of fundamental, hard-wired interests human beings have in love, death, adventure, family, justice, and adversity. These values counted as much in the Pleistocene as today, which is why they are so intensively studied by evolutionary psychologists.

Both Booker and Dutton are looking for ways of describing the coordinating mechanisms which allow individual agents not only to join the web of sense-making and hook up with other agents, but also to reduce the potential infinity of experience, semiosis and structures to order, and in the process to achieve 'self-actualization' (Abraham Maslow) if not 'self-realization' (Carl Jung). In other words, stories themselves are *organizing institutions* of language and of self, simultaneously. *They* 'speak' the bards, the media, the myriad individual storytellers, rather than the other way around.

A network characterized by growth and change is dynamic; a 'scale-free' network:

> As new nodes appear, they tend to connect to the more connected sites, and these popular locations thus acquire more links over time than their less connected neighbors. And this 'rich get richer' process will generally favor the early nodes, which are more likely eventually to become hubs. (Barabási and Bonabeau 2003: 55)

In the web of storytelling, Booker's seven basic plots are *hubs*, to which new events (plots) and agents (heroes) alike are 'preferentially attracted.' Thus new stories tend to end up like all the others:

1. Anticipation Stage – *The call* to adventure, and the promise of what is to come.
2. Dream Stage – The heroine or hero experiences some *initial success* – everything seems to be going well, sometimes with a dreamlike sense of invincibility (what we might call the 'Mission accomplished' stage).
3. Frustration Stage – First *confrontation* with the real enemy. Things begin to go wrong.
4. Nightmare Stage – At the point of maximum dramatic tension, disaster has erupted and it seems all hope is lost (*final ordeal*).
5. Resolution – The hero or heroine is eventually *victorious*, and may also be united or reunited with their 'other half' (a romantic partner).[10]

What is the benefit of reducing experience to such patterns? It may be that stories themselves are 'hard wired' to *enact* the sequence required for a new node to find productive links in a scale-free network. Stories are a *social technology* for passing on a model for how to navigate complex adaptive networks to succeeding generations. Stories are *about* how it feels and what it takes for a new 'node' to connect to a network, to navigate its topography, and to develop sufficient links to become a hub. There's a name for failure to connect too. Booker calls it 'tragedy.' And the name for characters who value *self* over *system*? Booker calls them 'evil.' Everything else is a version of Romance; they're all family dramas.

Narrative Reasoning

Here storytelling does what science cannot. Eric Beinhocker (2006: 126–7) reckons that stories are an evolutionary mechanism for *inductive reasoning*.

> As Plato said, 'Those who tell stories rule society.' . . . Stories are vital to us because the primary way we process information is through *induction*. Induction is essentially reasoning by pattern recognition . . . We like stories because they feed our induction

thinking machine, they give us material to find patterns in – stories are a way in which we learn.

Bearing in mind that this insight is offered in a book about complexity economics, it is as well to note that *learning* in this context is part of the answer to the question of how wealth is created, both long-term (evolutionary) and short-term (business success). Beinhocker is not celebrating the romance of the hero but seeking a scientific explanation for economic growth and an exact model for entrepreneurial action. In this context, learning has wealth-creating potential:

> Humans particularly excel at two aspects of inductive pattern recognition. The first is relating new experiences to old patterns, through metaphor and analogy-making ... Second, we are not just good pattern recognizers, but also very good pattern-completers. Our minds are experts at filling in the gaps of missing information. (Beinhocker, 2006: 127)

If Eric Beinhocker is right, and his is a very different model of 'economic rationalism' from that of traditional economics, then the stakes could hardly be higher. YouTube is a means for propagating this vehicle of inductive reasoning and learning to the outermost limit of the social; looking for ways to connect marginal, isolated, excluded or just shy 'nodes' so that they may thrive. He emphasizes that we need to understand the 'micro-behaviors of individuals' in order to understand how the system as a whole works:

> This model portrays humans as inductively rational pattern-recognizers who are able to make decisions in ambiguous and fast-changing environments and to learn over time. Real people are also neither purely self-regarding, nor purely altruistic. Rather, their behavior is attuned to eliciting cooperation in social networks, rewarding cooperation and punishing free riders. (Beinhocker, 2006: 138–9)

This is what YouTube teaches too. Beinhocker (2006: 141) goes on to say that 'networks are an essential ingredient in any complex adaptive system. Without interactions between agents, there can be no complexity.' In short, without such individual interactions, the entire system fails. So it behoves any progressive theory of communication to find a way to put the power of inductive reasoning – storytelling – where it belongs, in the minds and mouths of all agents, so that they may interact on a competitive footing, finding ways to 'access, understand and create communications in a variety of contexts,' as one national media regulator defines 'media literacy.'[11] Thence they may learn to navigate the 'hierarchies of networks within networks' (Beinhocker, 2006: 141) that characterize both markets in the global economy and meanings in the global sense-making system, including language, the Internet – and YouTube.

Notes

I HOW YOUTUBE MATTERS

1 A survey of the online video landscape circa 2005 is available on technology culture blog Techcrunch: www.techcrunch.com/2005/11/06/the-flickrs-of-video/

2 News Corporation, who had acquired MySpace the year before, were rumored to be bidders (Allison and Waters, 2006).

3 According to a Nielsen news release, available at: www.nielsen-netratings.com/pr/pr_071106_2_UK.pdf

4 At least according to both alexa.com and Nielsen data.

5 This figure is obtained by running a wildcard search within YouTube, using the universal wildcard expression "*". As of April 2008, this method no longer works to obtain a figure of the number of videos on the site.

6 http://www.comscore.com/press/release.asp?press=2223

7 http://slashdot.org/articles/05/08/14/1320217.shtml?tid=95&tid=129

8 Karim himself tells this story in a 2006 lecture at the University of Illinois at Urbana-Champaign, available on YouTube: http://www.youtube.com/watch?v=nssfmTo7SZg

9 The first video uploaded to the service was the humbly titled 'Me at the Zoo,' featuring Karim himself. This video is still available at: youtube.com/watch?v=jNQXAC9IVRw

10 http://www.youtube.com/press_room_entry?entry=vCfgHo5_Fb4; http://www.youtube.com/press_room_entry?entry=JrYdNx45e-0

2 YOUTUBE AND THE MAINSTREAM MEDIA

1 On the theory of 'labelling' and 'amplification' of social deviance, see Becker, 1963.

2 http://youtube.com/user/Beatbullying

3   http://www.thelonelyisland.com
4   http://youtube.com/mygrammymoment
5   http://youtube.com/fromheretoawesome
6   See the YouTube channel for the awards here http://youtube.com/
    Sketchies2
7   In part a response to John Hartley's (1999) discussion of the
    democratization of the media and the development of Do-It-Yourself
    citizenship.
8   See his video here http://youtube.com/watch?v=kHmvkRoEowc
9   Two good examples here are the humorists whatthebuck and sxephil.
10 http://youtube.com/watch?v=-_CS01gOd48
11 The vlog (short for 'video blog') is an extremely prevalent form of
    'amateur' video in YouTube. Typically structured primarily around
    a monologue delivered directly to camera, characteristically these
    videos are produced with little more than a webcam and some witty
    editing. The subject matter ranges from reasoned political debate to
    impassioned rants about YouTube itself and the mundane details of
    everyday life.
12 Heffernan's blog about television is available on the New York Times
    website at http://screens.blogs.nytimes.com/
13 According to the data presented in *PC Magazine*, YouTube's unique
    US Visitors jumped from 5,644 thousand in March 2006 to 12,669
    in May 2006, or an increase of around 124 percent.
14 Accessible from within the US at http://www.hulu.com
15 Viacom's amended complaint can be found here
    http://beckermanlegal.com/Documents/viacom_
    youtube_080418AmendedComplaint.pdf; YouTube's reply is
    available here http://beckermanlegal.com/Documents/viacom_yout
    ube_080523AnswertoAmendedComplaint.pdf
16 This is despite the fact the DMCA clearly places the burden of
    monitoring possibly infringing materials on the party claiming
    copyright ownership: http://www.nytimes.com/2007/03/18/
    opinion/18lessig.html
17 The press release is now off the web, but see the Mashable report on the
    filing of the suit: http://mashable.com/2007/03/13/viacom-youtube/

3 YOUTUBE'S POPULAR CULTURE

1   After the study had commenced YouTube introduced measures of
    popularity such as 'Most Active,' which would have added another
    layer of nuance to the sample.

2 Where videos were repeated in the sample, appearing in more than one category of popularity for instance, they were counted and coded individually, providing a sense of the extent and nature of material being watched and providing a sense of the weight of respective content types within YouTube.

3 The parameters of these categories were developed inductively, through the examination of subsets of the sample in combination with a process of discussion with the coders. They are not absolute nor are they exclusive – there is a degree of slippage between categories, and at a granular level, this survey doesn't achieve the degree of agreement between coders that would satisfy the requirements of a truly rigorous content analysis.

4 Users can navigate the site by category from the 'Videos' page, http://youtube.com/browse?s=mp

5 'Most Viewed' counts only full views and counts views from external embeds once per IP address according to tests run in 2007 by a video analytics company (TubeMogul, 2007).

6 Produced by professionals even if not necessarily from those working for large media corporations.

7 Produced by amateurs, often those without formal training or industrial support.

8 Where fans edit together footage from anime series to popular songs.

9 See Vidmeter.com's 2007 study of copyrighted videos on YouTube which reaches a similar conclusion about the videos removed from the service: http://www.vidmeter.com/i/vidmeter_copyright_report.pdf

10 When videos are marked by the uploader as 'private,' they are accessible only to invited guests.

11 However, as noted above, these removed videos were coded where possible, based on available information.

12 As of March 2008, the service is testing technology to increase the visual and audio quality of video on the site. See http://cybernetnews.com/2008/02/29/watch-high-resolution-youtube-videos/

13 The poor quality is due primarily to the compression technologies YouTube uses, though quality is also determined by a range of additional factors, such as the quality of the original recording and the technology used to digitize the content.

14 See YouTube's official response to this behavior on their blog: http://www.youtube.com/blog?entry=oorjVv_HDVs

15 We owe Sam Ford a debt of gratitude for suggesting the term for this particular practice.

16 Around two thirds of the Most Viewed videos were coded as traditional media content.

17 http://youtube.com/watch?v=LbkNxYaULBw
18 http://youtube.com/watch?v=GoLtUX_6IXY
19 Both of these videos were nominees for the 'Creative' category in the 2007 YouTube awards.
20 Though not organized into a channel of their own, these videos can be found by searching for 'YouTube Poop.' See for example http://youtube.com/watch?v=Lov8PTDmiEE
21 See, for example, 'Youtube poop: Nah-Roo-Toe paints on the faces of evil,' http://youtube.com/watch?v=I6Tr3dzuZ9U
22 The video 'Youtube Poop – LEAVE MAMA LUIGI ALONE!' at http://youtube.com/watch?v=5kG43D1elW0 uses clips from Chris Crocker's 'Leave Britney Alone' plea.
23 As discussed in the section on User-Led Innovation in the following chapter.
24 We owe Evan Wendal our gratitude for drawing to our attention the way this works.
25 Mia Rose's YouTube channel is available here http://youtube.com/user/miaarose
26 She was identified as both a 'user' and an independent producer by different coders.
27 http://youtube.com/user/unsw
28 http://youtube.com/user/ucberkeleycampuslife
29 The development team working on the Android mobile phone technology, for instance, uploads overviews of their progress. See http://youtube.com/view_play_list?p=D7C64411AF40DEA5
30 http://youtube.com/watch?v=czAaugp-S6I
31 http://youtube.com/user/fordmodels
32 'Changing Room Confessions: School Girl Look?' http://youtube.com/watch?v=fjfGE3ql_hc
33 http://youtube.com/user/nalts
34 http://youtube.com/user/charlestrippy
35 http://youtube.com/user/Blunty3000
36 http://www.viralvideofever.com

4 YOUTUBE'S SOCIAL NETWORK

 1 The Members page, available here http://youtube.com/members, provides a way to search the site according to which uploaders have been most watched or subscribed to.
 2 http://youtube.com/community
 3 http://stickam.com

4   See for example Chris Crocker's stickam profile: http://stickam. com/profile/itschriscrocker

5   The 12second.tv collaboration is available here http://12seconds. tv/channel/fantasticbabblings/9437 FantasticBabblings' longer vlog entry on the topic, here http://www.youtube.com/ watch?v=BBxjscfmon4

6   An example of a video-sharing site offering this feature is http:// viddler.com

7   The realization, for instance, that if you put an image of 'boobs' in the center frame of the video, you get more views.

8   'Mission Improbable: An Almost Shout-Out' is available here http:// youtube.com/watch?v=rV2tG9m_Pow

9   The Ofcom statement on media literacy is available from their website here http://www.ofcom.org.uk/advice/media_literacy/ of_med_lit/whatis/

10 Oakley's first video is available here http://youtube.com/watch?v=p_ YMigZmUuk

11 http://youtube.com/watch?v=jKJ8jRXNJJg

12 The video 'GTA sanandreas bike stunt,' by user jyumnai101 is a montage of stunts performed in the game *Grand Theft Auto: San Andreas* set music. The uploader is sure to point out in their description that the video, available here http://youtube.com/ watch?v=MF4H1Ut9jLU, features footage of players other than himself.

13 A number of users have uploaded montages of successful kills in first-person shooter game *Halo 3*. Many of these videos, such as 'Itwasluck :: Montage 7 :: Edited by Zola' available here http:// youtube.com/watch?v=YO7KMoNLl_Q, compile footage from other sources, such as videos posted to gameplay forums online. YouTube is as much a site to brag about your own abilities as it is to share, and marvel at, the skills of superior players.

14 Some users produce ongoing series' of such videos, such as CMNeir's 'Halo 3 Tricks: Episode 13 *The Invisible Warthog*,' available here http://youtube.com/watch?v=IVoq2hPJJu4.

5 YOUTUBE'S CULTURAL POLITICS

1   The invitation to respond to the question 'what does YOUR fridge say about YOU?' is available here http://youtube.com/ watch?v=sqduQT242Iw. This video is a good starting off point, as videos showing what is actually in the fridge are posted as responses.

The invitation is itself a response to a humorous vlog post by prominent YouTuber kevjumba discussing Asian stereotypes.

2 At least, data from the alexa.com web metrics service (which requires on an opt-in system via the toolbar and so may skew data in favor of more 'savvy' users) appear to indicate that the 'global' YouTube domain http://youtube.com is still far and away the most visited.

3 See for example the video 'YouTube Community Council – Great! But It's All White!' http://youtube.com/watch?v=BPJMzSy_wOg

4 YouTube's failure to 'penetrate' these markets, particularly in China, is a complex issue to do not only with 'censorship' but also to do with selective blocking and convenience for users, who tend to prefer local sites because of more reliable access as much as content relevance or loyalty. However, anecdotally it seems that YouTube is increasingly popular in Hong Kong and Taiwan where there is a traditional Chinese language/localization version of YouTube.

5 The *YouTube Stars* blog post discussing Oprah's arrival on YouTube is available here http://youtubestars.blogspot.com/2007/11/oprah-is-on-youtube.html

6 The 'Nalts on Oprah? Noprah,' video is available here http://youtube.com/watch?v=c_ZNVESIwGw

7 Renetto's video is here http://youtube.com/watch?v=IYRucYmDsMo

8 Paperlilies' vlog post is available here http://youtube.com/watch?v=Jko5NZUqVZo

9 The *YouTube Stars* most viewed list is available here http://www.bkserv.net/YTS/YTMostViewed.aspx

10 This video has since been removed.

6 YOUTUBE'S UNCERTAIN FUTURES

1 Random Brainwave discuss the hoax here http://randombrainwave.blogspot.com/2008/01/world-gets-brainwavd.html

2 Channel 4's story is available here http://youtube.com/watch?v=sQgg7SIWppo

3 Fox's 'The Blast' episode featuring the story is available here http://youtube.com/watch?v=Hnls6FocNy4

4 In *Bureaucracy*, Honore de Balzac (1891) describes 'the egotist' as 'sharp, aggressive, and indiscreet, he did mischief for mischief's sake; above all, he attacked the weak, respected nothing and believed in nothing . . .' While infinitely more playful and less malevolent than the egotism Balzac describes, the idea of 'mischief

for mischief's sake' at least is an oddly apt description of Corey
Delaney's media persona and the discourses employed by his
swarm of 'supporters.'

5 Full details, background and transcripts are available at a special
section of the ABC website: http://www.abc.net.au/news/events/
apology/

6 Blog entries from attendees at YouTube's recent talks to advertisers
and corporate partners at least gesture in this direction.

7 http://groups.google.com/group/youtube-help

8 TeacherTube is at http://www.teachertube.com/

9 Story Circles is at http://storycircles.org/

WHAT HAPPENED BEFORE YOUTUBE

1 http://www.thehpalliance.org/

2 'Harry Potter and the Dark Lord Waldemart,' http://youtube.com/
watch?v=nooWqYWdH74

3 http://www.imeem.com/

4 See for instance, the Archive of Our Own project: http://
transformativeworks.org/projects/archive.html

5 This mission is developed and articulated online at http://
transformativeworks.org/faq/

6 http://youtube.com/watch?v=IZSqXUSwHRI

USES OF YOUTUBE: DIGITAL LITERACY AND THE
GROWTH OF KNOWLEDGE

1 Chief investigators on YIRN were John Hartley and Greg Hearn,
with researchers Jo Tacchi and Tanya Notley. YIRN was funded as an
Australian Research Council 'Linkage' project with Arts Queensland,
Brisbane City Council, Queensland Office of Youth Affairs and
Music Queensland as partners (see Hartley et al., 2003).

2 Most Australian states ban school use of YouTube to resist
'cyber-bullying': see http://www.australianit.news.com.au/
story/0,24897,21330109-15306,00.html. For an interesting
discussion of the pedagogy of banning Internet affordances
in university teaching, see: http://www.theargus.co.uk/news/
generalnews/display.var.1961862.0.lecturer_bans_students_from_
using_google_and_wikipedia.php

3 http://youtube.com/watch?v=-_CS01gOd48

4 See http://youtube.com/user/lonelygirl15; see also the entry in the Wikipedia, which claims over 70 million combined views for LG15 on various platforms (September 2007), including YouTube, Revver, metacafe, LiveVideo, Veoh, Bebo, and MySpace.

5 See http://youtube.com/watch?v=l6z6oGWzbkA

6 Some cultural scientists dispute Barabási's concept of preferential attachment, preferring a model of random copying. See Alex Bentley and Stephen Shennan (2005) 'Random copying and cultural evolution.' *Science*, vol. 309, 5 August: 877–9. YouTube may be a 'live experiment' to test these different explanations for how social networks evolve.

7 Searching "mission accomplished" on YouTube yielded nearly 900 videos (April 2008). See for instance: http://youtube.com/watch?v=-GJUGUYsm68 (ABC News story previewing the speech); and http://youtube.com/watch?v=lIfjmr-Kmxk&feature=related (re-versioned footage from USS Lincoln).

8 For the full speech on YouTube see: http://youtube.com/watch?v=faMTYPYfDSE&feature=related; and: http://youtube.com/watch?v=oz9RIjGWpJk&feature=related (the section quoted in this chapter is on the second clip). See also http://www.whitehouse.gov/news/releases/2003/05/20030501-15.html

9 See also Michiko Kakutani (2005) 'The Plot Thins, or Are No Stories New?' *New York Times* 15 April. accessible at: http://www.nytimes.com/2005/04/15/books/15book.html

10 Adapted from a detailed and dispassionate account of Booker's ideas by Chris Bateman at his blog *Only a Game*: http://onlyagame.typepad.com/only_a_game/2005/10/the_seven_basic.html

11 The British media regulator, Ofcom, has a statutory duty to promote media literacy among the UK population. Its definition of media literacy was arrived at after extensive consultation: 'Media literacy is the ability to access, understand and create communications in a variety of contexts.' See: http://www.ofcom.org.uk/consult/condocs/strategymedialit/ml_statement/; and for the full range of Ofcom's media literacy reports see: http://www.ofcom.org.uk/advice/media_literacy/medlitpub/medlitpubrss/.

References

'Best YouTube Videos' (2007) *A Current Affair*. Nine Network, Australia, 31 December.

'Premier League to take action against YouTube' (2007) *Telegraph Online*, 23 May. Available at: http://www.telegraph.co.uk/sport/football/2312532/Premier-League-to-take-action-against-YouTube.html

'Teachers in Website Closure Call' (2007) *BBC.co.uk*, 1 August. Available at: http://news.bbc.co.uk/2/hi/uk_news/scotland/6925444.stm

'The TV Net Arrives' (2006) *PC Magazine*, 22 August, p. 19.

'UPDATE 2-Mediaset sues Google, YouTube; seeks $780 mln' (2008) Reuters-UK, 30 July: Available at: http://uk.reuters.com/article/governmentFilingsNews/idUKL04549520080730

'YouTube's Most Watched' (2007) *Today Tonight*. Seven Network, Australia, 31 December.

'YouTube's Greatest Hits With The Billionaire Founders' (2007) *The Oprah Winfrey Show*. Available at: http://www.oprah.com/tows/pastshows/200711/tows_past_20071106.jhtml

'YouTube Tackles Bullying Online' (2007) *BBC.co.uk*, 19 November. Available at: http://news.bbc.co.uk/1/hi/education/7098978.stm

Adegoke, Yinka (2006a) 'PluggedIn: New rock stars use Web videos to win fans.' *Reuters News*, 25 August. Accessed via Factiva database.

— (2006b) 'YouTube video to fly free under Google's wing.' *Reuters News*, 10 October. Accessed via Factiva database.

Albrechtslund, Anders (2008) 'Online Social Networking as Participatory Surveillance.' *First Monday* 13(3): Available at: http://www.uic.edu/htbin/cgiwrap/bin/ojs/index.php/fm/article/viewArticle/2142/1949

Alexander, Harriet (2007), 'Lectures Online for YouTube Generation.' *The Sydney Morning Herald*, Sydney, 7 November. Accessed via Factiva database.

Allison, Kevin (2006) 'YouTube Content with Video Presence Online.' *Financial Times*, London, 10 April, p. 24.

Allison, Kevin and Chris Nuttall (2006) 'YouTube Deal a Catalyst for Online Video.' *Financial Times*, London, 12 October. Accessed via Factiva database.

Allison, Kevin and Aline Van Duyn (2006) 'Google Agrees Dollars: 1.65bn Deal for YouTube.' *Financial Times*, London, 10 October. Accessed via Factiva database.

Allison, Kevin and Richard Waters, (2006) 'Google and Murdoch Among the Suitors Circling YouTube.' *Financial Times*, London, 7 October. Accessed via Factiva database.

Andersen, Robin (2006) *A Century of Media, A Century of War*. New York: Peter Lang.

Andrejevic, Mark (2003) *Reality TV: The Work of Being Watched*. Lanham, MD: Rowman and Littlefield.

— (2005) 'The Work of Watching One Another: Lateral Surveillance, Risk, and Governance.' *Surveillance & Society* 2(4): 479–97.

Arrington, Michael (2005a) 'Profile – YouTube.' *TechCrunch*, 8 August. Available at: http://www.techcrunch.com/2005/08/08/profile-you tube/

— (2005b) 'Comparing the Flickrs of Video.' *TechCrunch*, 6 November. Available at: http://www.techcrunch.com/2005/11/06/the-flickrs-of-video/

Arthur, Charles (2006) 'Has YouTube changed since its purchase this month by Google?' *The Guardian*, London, 26 October. Accessed via Factiva database.

Atton, Chris (2002) *Alternative Media*. London: Sage.

Aufderheide, Pat, and Peter Jaszi (2008) *Recut, Reframe, Recycle: Quoting Copyrighted Material in User-Generated Video* (January). Washington University: Center for Social Media, American University. Available at: http://www.centerforsocialmedia.org/recut

Balzac, Honoré de (1891) *Bureaucracy: Or, a Civil Service Reformer (Les Employés)*. Balzac's Novels in English (Vol.11). London: Routledge.

Baker, Sarah Louise (2004) 'Pop in(to) the Bedroom: Popular Music in Pre-Teen Girls' Bedroom Culture.' *European Journal of Cultural Studies* 7(1): 75–93.

Banks, John (2002) 'Gamers as Co-Creators: Enlisting the Virtual Audience – a Report From the Net Face.' *Mobilising the Audience*. Eds Mark Balnaves, Tom O'Regan, and Jason Sternberg. Brisbane: University of Queensland Press, pp. 188–213.

Banks, John and Sal Humphreys (2008) 'The Labour of User Co-Creators: Emergent Social Network Markets?' *Convergence: The International Journal of Research into New Media Technologies* 14(4): 401–18.

Barabási, Albert-László (2002) *Linked: How Everything is Connected to Everything Else*. Cambridge, MA: Perseus.

Barabási, Albert-László and Eric Bonabeau (2003) 'Scale-free Networks.' *Scientific American*, May: 50–9.

Bawden Tom and Dan Sabbagh (2006) 'Google to buy YouTube for $1.65bn.' *The Times*, London, 10 October, p. 53.

Becker, Anne (2007) 'YouTube to Viacom: We Will Pull Your Clips.' *Broadcasting and Cable*, 2 February.

Becker, Howard S. (1963) *Outsiders: Studies in the Sociology of Deviance*. London, New York: Free Press of Glencoe.

— (1982) *Art Worlds*. Berkeley: University of California Press.

Beinhocker, Eric (2006) *The Origin of Wealth: Evolution, Complexity and the Radical Remaking of Economics*, NY and London: Random House.

Benkler, Yochai (2006) *The Wealth of Networks: How Social Production Transforms Markets and Freedom*. New Haven and London: Yale University Press.

Benson, Simon (2007) 'YouTube Law to Shame Hoons.' *Daily Telegraph*, Sydney, 12 November. Available at: http://www.news.com.au/

Bentley, Alex and Stephen Shennan, (2005) "Random Copying and Cultural Evolution." *Science* 309, 5 August: 877–9.

Biggs, John (2006) 'A Video Clip Goes Viral, and a TV Network Wants to Control It.' *New York Times*, New York, 20 February. Available at: http://www.nytimes.com/

Blakely, Rhys (2007) 'YouTube fails to satisfy critics over copyright.' *The Times*, London. 17 October, p. 49.

Bonner, Frances (2003) *Ordinary Television: Analyzing Popular TV*. London: Sage.

Booker, Christopher (2004) *The Seven Basic Plots: Why We Tell Stories*. London: Continuum.

Bovill, Moira and Sonia Livingstone (2001) 'Bedroom Culture and the Privatization of Media Use.' *Children and Their Changing Media Environment: A European Comparative Study*. Mahwah, NJ: Lawrence Earlbaum Associates, pp. 179–200.

boyd, danah (2007) 'Why Youth (Heart) Social Network Sites: The Role of Networked Publics in Teenage Social Life.' *MacArthur Foundation Series on Digital Learning – Youth, Identity, and Digital Media Volume*. Ed. David Buckingham. Cambridge, MA: MIT Press

boyd, danah m. and Nicole B. Ellison (2007) 'Social Network Sites: Definition, History, and Scholarship.' *Journal of Computer-Mediated Communication* 13(1): 210–30. Available at: http://jcmc.indiana.edu/vol13/issue1/boyd.ellison.html

Branwyn, Gareth (1997) *Jamming the Media: A Citizen's Guide: Reclaiming the Tools of Communication*. Chronicle Books.

Broersma, Matthew (2007) 'Viacom to YouTube: Take Down Pirated Clips.' *ZDNet*, 2 February. Available at: http://news.zdnet.com/2100-9595-6155771.html

Brooker, Will (2002) *Using the Force: Creativity, Community and Star Wars Fans*. New York: Continuum International Publishing Group Inc.

Bruns, Axel (2007) 'Produsage, Generation C, and Their Effects on the Democratic Process', Paper presented at *MiT 5 (Media in Transition) Conference*, MIT, Boston, USA, 27–9 April 2007. Available at: http://snurb.info/publications

— (2008) *Blogs, Wikipedia, Second Life, and Beyond: From Production to Produsage*. New York: Peter Lang.

Bruno, Antony (2007) 'The YouTube Conundrum', *Billboard*, 3 March. Accessed via Factiva database.

Burgess, Jean (2006) 'Hearing Ordinary Voices: Cultural Studies, Vernacular Creativity and Digital Storytelling.' *Continuum: Journal of Media & Cultural Studies* 2(20): 201–14.

— (2007) *Vernacular Creativity and New Media*. PhD Dissertation, Queensland University of Technology. Available at: http://eprints.qut.edu.au/archive/00010076/

Butsch, Richard (2000) *The Making of American Audiences: From Stage to Television, 1750–1990*. Cambridge: Cambridge University Press.

Butterfield, Stewart (2006) "Eyes of the World." *FlickrBlog*. Available at <http://blog.flickr.com/flickrblog/2006/03/eyes_of_the_wor.html>

Byrne, Seamus (2005) 'Be seen, read, heard.' *The Sydney Morning Herald*, Sydney, 3 September, p. 4.

Callon, Michel (1998) 'Introduction: The Embeddedness of Economic Markets in Economics.' *The Laws of the Markets*. Ed. Michel Callon. Oxford: Blackwell, pp. 1–57.

Campbell, Joseph (1949) *The Hero With a Thousand Faces*. Princeton NJ: Princeton University Press.

Cascio, James (2005). 'The Rise of the Participatory Panopticon.' *World Changing*. 4 May. Available at: http://www.worldchanging.com/archives/002651.html

Cha, Meeyoung, Haewoon Kwak, Pablo Rodriguez, Yong-Yeol Ahn, and Sue Moon (2007) 'I Tube, You Tube, Everybody Tubes: Analyzing the World's Largest User Generated Content Video System.' Paper presented at *IMC'07: Internet Measurement Conference*, San Diego, CA.

Charny, Ben (2007) 'YouTube Gave User's Data To Paramount's Lawyers.' *Dow Jones News Service*, 21 October. Accessed via Factiva database.

Chonin, Neva (2006) 'Who's That Girl?' *San Francisco Chronicle*, 3 September, p. 14.

Cohen, Stanley (1972) *Folk Devils and Moral Panics: The Creation of the Mods and Rockers*. London: MacGibbon and Kee.

Collins, James and Richard K. Blot (2003) *Literacy and Literacies: Texts, Power, and Identity*. Cambridge: Cambridge University Press.

Consalvo, Mia (2003) 'Cyber-Slaying Media Fans: Code, Digital Poaching, and Corporate Control of the Internet.' *Journal of Communication Inquiry* 27(1): 67–86.

Conti, Cynthia (2001). *'Stepping Up to the Mic': Le Tigre Strategizes Third Wave Feminist Activism Through Music and Performance.* Masters Thesis in Comparative Media Studies, MIT. Available online: http://cms.mit.edu/research/theses/CynthiaConti2001.pdf

Coppa, Francesca (2007). 'Celebrating Candy Fong: Founder of Fannish Music Video.' *In Media Res,* 19 November. Available from: http://mediacommons.futureofthebook.org/videos/

Couldry, Nick (2000) *The Place of Media Power: Pilgrims and Witnesses of the Media Age.* London and New York: Routledge.

— (2003) *Media Rituals: A Critical Approach.* London and New York: Routledge.

— (2006) *Listening Beyond the Echoes: Media, Ethics and Agency in an Uncertain World.* Boulder, CO: Paradigm.

Couldry, Nick and Tim Markham (2007) 'Celebrity Culture and Public Connection: Bridge Or Chasm?' *International Journal of Cultural Studies* 10(4): 403–21.

Coyle, Jake (2006) 'YouTube Community Fears They Will be Pushed Out.' *Associated Press Newswires,* 12 October. Accessed via Factiva database.

Crystal, David (2005) *English as a Global Language.* 2nd edn Cambridge: Cambridge University Press.

Cunningham, Stuart and Tina Nguyen (2000) 'Popular Media of the Vietnamese Diaspora.' *Floating Lives: The Media and Asian Diasporas.* Eds Stuart Cunningham and John Sinclair. St Lucia, Queensland, University of Queensland Press, pp. 91–135.

Dash, Anil (1999) 'Last Refuge of the Parentheticals?' *Anil Dash Blog,* 15 August. Available at: www.dashes.com/anil/1999/08/last-refuge-of.html

Davis, Joshua (2006) 'The Secret World of Lonelygirl.' *Wired,* 14(12): 232–9.

Davis, Marc (1997) 'Garage Cinema and The Future of Media Technology.' *Communications of the ACM (50th Anniversary Edition Invited Article)* 40 (2): 42–8.

De Certeau, Michel (1984) *The Practice of Everyday Life.* Trans. Steven F. Rendal. Vol. 1. Berkeley: University of California Press.

Delaney, Kevin J. (2006) 'Garage Brand: With NBC Pact, YouTube Site Tries to Build a Lasting Business.' *The Wall Street Journal,* 27 June, p. A1.

Delaney, Kevin J. (2008) "Google Push To Sell Ads On YouTube Hits Snags – Video Site Is Key To Diversification; The Lawsuit Factor." *Wall Street Journal,* New York, 9 July, p. A.1.

Delaney, Kevin J. and Matthew Karnitschnig, (2007) "Reception Problems: TV Industry Clouds Google's Video Vision; Tensions Are Rising Over

YouTube Postings; CBS Talks Go Off Track." *Wall Street Journal,* New York, 21 February, p. A.1.

De Vreese, Claes H. (2005) 'News Framing: Theory and Typology.' *Information Design Journal* 13(1): 51–62.

Deuze, Mark (2007) *Media Work.* Cambridge: Polity.

Dilanian, Ken (2007) 'YouTube makes leap into politics.' *USA Today,* 23 July. Accessed via Factiva database.

Driscoll, Catherine and Melissa Gregg (2008) 'Broadcast Yourself: Moral Panic, Youth Culture and Internet Studies.' *Youth, Media and Culture in the Asia Pacific Region.* Eds Usha M. Rodrigues and Belinda Smaill. Newcastle: Cambridge Scholars Publishing, pp. 71–86.

Drotner, Kirsten (1999) 'Dangerous Media? Panic Discourses and Dilemmas of Modernity.' *Paedagogica Historica* 35(3): 593–619.

— (2000) 'Difference and Diversity: Trends in Young Danes' Media Uses.' *Media, Culture & Society* 22(2): 149–66.

— (2008) 'Leisure is Hard Work: Digital Practices and Future Competencies.' *Youth, Identity, and Digital Media.* Ed. David Buckingham. The John D. And Catherine T. Macarthur Foundation Series on Digital Media and Learning. Cambridge, MA: The MIT Press, pp. 167–84.

Duncombe, Stephen (1997) *Notes From Underground: Zines And The Politics Of Alternative Culture.* London, New York: Verso

Dutton, Dennis (2005) 'Upon a Time.' *The Washington Post,* 8 May. Available at: www.washingtonpost.com/wp-dyn/content/article/2005/05/05/AR 2005050501385_pf.html

Eason, Kevin (2008) 'Ministers Go Surfing in Hope of Catching Kids in their Net.' *The Times,* London, 13 March, p. 87.

Elfman, Doug (2006) 'Wag of the Finger at YouTube.' *The Chicago Sun-Times,* Chicago, 31 October. Accessed via Factiva database.

Elias, Paul (2006) 'Google Reportedly Talking With YouTube.' *Associated Press Newswires,* 7 October. Accessed via Factiva database.

Feldman, Claudia (2007) 'A Turning Point in Politics?' *The Houston Chronicle,* Houston, 25 July. Accessed via Factiva database.

Fine, Jon (2006) 'The Strange Case of lonelygirl15.' *Business Week,* 11 September, p. 22.

Fischer, Claude S. (1992) *America Calling: A Social History of the Telephone to 1940.* Berkeley: University of California Press.

Fiske, John (1989) *Reading the Popular.* Boston: Unwin Hyman.

— (1992a) *Understanding Popular Culture,* London and New York: Routledge.

— (1992b) 'The Cultural Economy of Fandom.' *The Adoring Audience: Fan Culture and Popular Media.* Ed. Lisa A. Lewis. London: Routledge, pp. 30–49.

Fiske, John and John Hartley (2003 [1978]) *Reading Television*. Revised edn London: Routledge.

Frith, Simon (1996) 'Music and Identity.' *Cultural Identity*. Eds Stuart Hall and Paul du Gay. London and Thousand Oaks, Sage Publications Ltd, pp. 108–27.

Galloway, Anne, Jonah Brucker-Cohen, Lalya Gaye and Elizabeth Goodman (2004) 'Panel: Design for Hackability.' *Designing Interactive Systems (DIS2004)*. Available at: http://www.sigchi.org/DIS2004/Documents/Panels/DIS2004_Design_for_Hackability.pdf

Gandy, Oscar H. (2002) "The Real Digital Divide: Citizens Versus Consumers." *Handbook of New Media: Social Shaping and Consequences of ICTs*. Eds Leah A Lievrouw and Sonia Livingstone. London: Sage, pp. 448–60.

Gannes, Liz. (2006) 'Jawed Karim: How YouTube Took Off.' *Gigacom*. 26 October. Available at: http://gigaom.com/2006/10/26/jawed-karim-how-youtube-took-off/

Geek Community, The (2008). 'The Geek Community Manifesto.' *Headphone Sacriment*. http://tsuibhne.net/the-geek-culture-manifesto/

Gehl, Robert (2009) 'YouTube *As* Archive: Who Will Curate this Digital *Wunderkammer?*' *International Journal of Cultural Studies* 12(1): 43–160.

Gell, Alfred (1998) *Art and Agency: An Anthropological Theory*. Oxford: Oxford University Press.

Geist, Michael (2006) 'Why YouTube Won't Become Napster Redux.' *The Toronto Star*, Toronto, 16 October, p. C3.

Gentile, G (2006) 'Online Mystery of Video-Diary Posting by "Lonelygirl15" Continues to Deepen.' *Associated Press Newswires*, 11 September. Accessed via Factiva database.

Gill, Phillipa, Martin Arlitt, Li Zongpeng, and Anirban Mahanti (2007) 'YouTube Traffic Characterization: A View From the Edge.' Paper presented at *IMC'07*, San Diego, CA.

Goetz, Thomas (2005) 'Reinventing Television.' *Wired* 13(9). Available at: http://www.wired.com/wired/archive/13.09/stewart.html

Goo, Sara Kehaulani (2006) 'Ready for its Close-Up; With Google Said to be a Suitor, YouTube Enters Mainstream.' *The Washington Post*, 7 October, p. D1.

Gracy, Karen F. (2007) 'Moving Image Preservation and Cultural Capital.' *Library Trends* 56(1): 183–98.

Graham, Jefferson (2005) 'Video websites pop up, invite postings; Digital cameras spread capability.' *USA Today*, National, 22 November, p. B3.

Gray, Jonathan, Cornel Sandvoss, and C. Lee Harrington (2008) 'Introduction: Why Study Fans?' *Fandom: Identities and Communities in a Media World.* Eds Jonathan Gray, Cornell, Sandvoss and C. Lee Harrington. New York and London: New York University Press, pp. 1–16.

Green, Joshua (2008) 'Why Do They Call it TV When It's Not On the Box? 'New' Television Services and 'Old' Television Functions.' *Media International Australia Incorporating Culture and Policy* 126 (February): 95–105.

Green, Joshua and Henry Jenkins (2009) 'The Moral Economy of Web 2.0: Audience Research and Convergence Culture.' *Media Industries: History, Theory and Methods.* Eds Jennifer Holt and Alisa Perren. Chichester/Oxford: Wiley.

Greenberg, Dan (2007) 'The Secret Strategies Behind Many 'Viral' Videos.' *TechCrunch.* Available at:http://techcrunch.com/2007/11/22/the-secret-strategies-behind-many-viral-videos/

Grossman, Lev (2006a) 'How to Get Famous in 30 Seconds.' *TIME.* Available at http://time.com/time/magazine/article/0,9171,1184060,00.html

— (2006b) 'Time's Person of the Year: You.' *TIME.* Available at: http://time.com/time/magazine/article/0,9171,1569514,00.html

Habermas, Jürgen (1989) *The Structural Transformation of the Public Sphere: An Inquiry Into a Category of Bourgeois Society.* Cambridge: Polity.

Hall, Stuart (1980) 'Cultural Studies: Two Paradigms.' *Media, Culture & Society* 2, pp. 57–72.

— (1981) 'Notes on Deconstructing "the Popular".' *People's History and Socialist Theory.* Ed. Raphael Samuel. London: Routledge and Kegan Paul, pp. 227–39.

Hall, Stuart, *et al.* (1978) *Policing the Crisis: Mugging, the State, and Law and Order.* London: Macmillan.

Harley, D. and G. Fitzpatrick (2008) 'YouTube and Intergenerational Communication: The Case of Geriatric1927.' *Universal Access in the Information Society:* (forthcoming).

Harris, John (2006) 'The Vision Thing.' *The Guardian,* London, 11 October, p. 6.

Harris, Neil (1973). *Humbug: The Art of P.T. Barnum.* Chicago: The University of Chicago Press.

Hartley, John (1999) *Uses of Television.* London: Routledge.

— (2004) 'The "Value Chain of Meaning" and the New Economy.' *International Journal of Cultural Studies* 1(7): 129–41.

— (2008a) *Television Truths: Forms of Knowledge in Popular Culture.* London: Blackwell.

— (2008b) '"Numbers Over Knowledge"? Journalism and Popular Culture.' *Handbook of Journalism Studies.* Eds Karin Wahl-Jorgensen and Thomas Hanitzsch. Mahwah, NJ: Lawrence Erlbaum Associates, forthcoming 2009. Author version cited.

— (2008c) 'TV Stories – From the 'Bardic function' to the 'Eisteddfod function.' *Story Circle: Digital Storytelling Around the World*. Eds John Hartley and Kelly McWilliam. Oxford: Blackwell.

— (2009) 'From the Consciousness Industry to Creative Industries: Consumer-Created Content, Social Network Markets and the Growth of Knowledge.' *Media Industries: History, Theory and Methods*. Eds Jennifer Holt and Alisa Perren. Oxford: Blackwell.

Hartley, John, Greg Hearn, Jo Tacchi and Marcus Foth (2003) 'The Youth Internet Radio Network: A Research Project to Connect Youth Across Queensland Through Music, Creativity and ICT.' In S. Marshall and W. Taylor (eds). *Proceedings of the 5th International Information Technology in Regional Areas (ITiRA) Conference 2003*. Rockhampton, QLD: Central Queensland University Press, pp. 335–42.

Hastie, David (2008), 'Web Invite Sees Party Explode into Drunken Rampage.' *The Courier Mail*, Brisbane, 14 January. Accessed via Factiva Database.

Hawkes, Terence (1977) *Structuralism and Semiotics*. London: Methuen.

Heath, Stephen (1990) 'Representing Television.' *Logics of television: essays in cultural criticism*. Ed. Patricia Mellencamp. London: BFI and Indiana: Indiana University Press, pp. 267–302.

Hebdige, D. (1988) *Hiding in the Light: On Images and Things*. London: Routledge.

Heffernan, Virginia and Tom Zeller Jr. (2006) 'Well, It Turns Out That Lonelygirl Really Wasn't.' *The New York Times*, New York, 13 September. Accessed via Factiva database.

Helft, Miguel (2007) 'Google Aims to Make YouTube Profitable With Ads.' *The New York Times*. 22 August. Available at: http://www.nytimes.com/2007/08/22/technology/22google.html

— (2008) 'Google Told to Turn Over User Data of YouTube.' *The New York Times*. 4 July. Available at: http://www.nytimes.com/2008/07/04/technology/04youtube.html

Hellekson, Karen and Kristina Busse, eds (2006) *Fan Fiction and Fan Communities in the Age of the Internet: New Essays*. Jefferson, N.C: McFarland & Co.

Hermes, Joke (2005) *Re-Reading Popular Culture*. Malden: Blackwell.

— (2006) 'Hidden Debates: Rethinking the Relationship Between Popular Culture and the Public Sphere.' *Javnost – The Public* 13(4): 27–44.

Herring, Susan C. (2008) 'Questioning the Generational Divide: Technological Exoticism and Adult Constructions of Online Youth Identity.' *Youth, Identity, and Digital Media*. Ed. David Buckingham. The John D. And Catherine T. Macarthur Foundation Series on Digital Media and Learning. Cambridge, MA: The MIT Press, pp. 71–92.

Hilderbrand, Lucas (2007) 'Youtube: Where Cultural Memory and Copyright Converge.' *Film Quarterly* 61(1): 48–57.

Hill, Logan (2007) 'The Vidder: Luminosity Upgrades Fan Video.' *New York Magazine*, 12 November. Available at: http://nymag.com/movies/features/videos/40622/

Hobbs, Renée (1998) 'The Seven Great Debates in the Media Literacy Movement.' *Journal of Communication* 48(1): 6–32.

Hof, Karina (2006) 'Something You Can Actually Pick Up: Scrapbooking as a Form and Forum of Cultural Citizenship.' *European Journal of Cultural Studies* 3(9): 363–84.

Hoggart, Richard (1957) *The Uses of Literacy*. Harmondsworth: Penguin.

Hughes, Gary (2008) '500 Teens Rampage as Police End Party.' *The Australian*, 14 January. Accessed via Factiva database.

Humphreys, Sal (2005a) 'Productive Players: Online Computer Games' Challenge to Conventional Media Forms.' *Journal of Communication and Critical/Cultural Studies* 1(2): 36–50.

— (2005b) 'Productive Users, Intellectual Property and Governance: The Challenges of Computer Games.' *Media and Arts Law Review* 10(4): 229–310.

Hurley, Chad (2007) 'You Too.' *Forbes*, 7 May, pp. 68–70.

Hutchinson, Bill (2007) 'YouTube Hails Web Wonders', *New York Daily News*. 27 March. Accessed via Factiva database.

Hyde, Lewis (2007 [1979]) *The Gift: How The Creative Spirit Transforms The World*. 25th anniversary edn. 2nd Vintage Books edn. New York: Vintage Books.

Ivey, Bill and Steven J. Tepper (2006) 'Cultural Renaissance or Cultural Divide?' *The Chronicle of Higher Education*, 19 May, p. B6.

Jakobson, Roman (1958) 'Closing Statement: Linguistics and Poetics.' *Style and Language*. Ed. Thomas A. Sebeok (1960). Cambridge, MA: MIT Press, pp. 350–77.

Jarrett, Kylie (2008) 'Beyond Broadcast Yourself™: The Future of YouTube.' *Media International Australia* 126: 132–44.

Jenkins, Henry (1992) *Textual Poachers: Television Fans and Participatory Culture*. New York and London: Routledge.

— (2006a) *Convergence Culture: Where Old and New Media Collide*. New York: New York University Press.

— (2006b) *Fans, Bloggers and Gamers: Exploring Participatory Culture*. New York: New York University Press.

— (2006c) 'YouTube and the Vaudeville Aesthetic.' *Confessions of an Aca-Fan*. 20 November. Available at: http://www.henryjenkins.org/2006/11/youtube_and_the_vaudeville_aes.html

— (2007) 'Are You Hep to That Jive?': The Fan Culture Surrounding Swing

Music.' *Confessions of an Aca-Fan.* 31 January. Available at: http://henryjenkins.org/2007/01/are_you_hep_the_fan_culture_su.html

— (2008a) 'Learning Through YouTube: An Interview with Alex Juhasz.' *Confessions of an Aca-Fan.* 20 February. Available at: http://henryjenkins.org/2008/02/learning_from_youtube_an_inter.html

— (2008b) 'From Rodney King to Burma: An Interview with Witness's Sam Gregory.' *Confessions of an Aca-Fan.* 31 March. Available at: http://henryjenkins.org/2008/03/from_rodney_king_to_burma_an_i.html

— (forthcoming) 'Why Mitt Romney Won't Debate A Snowman.'

Jenkins, Henry, Tara McPherson, and Jane Shattuc (2002) 'The Culture That Sticks to Your Skin: A Manifesto for a New Cultural Studies,' in *Hop on Pop: The Politics and Pleasures of Popular Culture*, Henry Jenkins, Tara McPherson and Jane Shattuc (eds). Durham, NC: Duke University Press, pp. 1–3.

Jenkins, Henry, Ravi Purushotma, Katie Clinton, Margaret Weigel and Alice J. Robison (2006) *Confronting the Challenges of Participatory Culture Media Education for the 21st Century.* Chicago: MacArthur Foundation.

Jenson, Joli (1992) 'Fandom as Pathology: The Consequences of Characterization.' *The Adoring Audience: Fan Culture and Popular Media.* Ed. Lisa A. Lewis. London: Routledge, pp. 9–29.

Jones, Sandra (2007) 'Wal-Mart Cast as Dark Lord.' *Chicago Tribune.* 1 July.

Johnson, Derek (2007) 'Inviting Audiences In: The spatial reorganization of production and consumption in "TVIII".' *New Review of Film and Television Studies* 5(1): 61–80.

Karnitschnig, Matthew (2007) 'New Viacom deal takes swipe at YouTube,' *The Wall Street Journal,* 20 February, p. B12. Accessed via Factiva database.

Karnitschnig, Matthew and Kevin Delaney (2006) 'Media Titans Pressure YouTube Over Copyrights.' *The Wall Street Journal,* 14 October, p. A3. Accessed via Factiva database.

Karpovich, Angelina I. (2007) 'Reframing Fan Videos.' *Music, Sound and Multimedia: From the Live to the Virtual.* Ed. Jamie Sexton. Edinburgh: Edinburgh University Press, pp. 17–28.

Keen, Andrew (2007) *The Cult of the Amateur: How Today's Internet is Killing Our Culture.* New York: Random House.

Kerwin, Ann Marie (2006) 'NBC Doesn't Believe in Viral.' *Advertising Age* 77(9): 51.

Kessler, Andy (2007) 'YouTube U.' *The Weekly Standard.* 29 October. Accessed via Factiva database.

Kirsner, Scott (2005) 'Now Playing: Your Home Video.' *The New York Times,* New York, 27 October. Accessed via Factiva database.

Knight, Brooke A. (2000) 'Watch Me! Webcams and the Public Exposure of Private Lives.' *Art Journal* 59(4): 21–5.

Kopytoff, Verne (2006). 'Copyright questions dog YouTube / Deals with entertainment industry limit site's liability.' *The San Francisco Chronicle*, San Francisco, 27 October, p. D1.

Kornblum, Janet (2006) 'Now Playing on YouTube.' *USA Today*, 18 July. Available at: http://www.usatoday.com/tech/news/2006-07-17-digital-download-youtube_x.htm

Koskela, Hille (2004) 'Webcams, TV Shows and Mobile Phones: Empowering Exhibitionism.' *Surveillance & Society* 2(2/3): 199–215.

Kranz, Cindy (2008) 'Schools take stance on bullying: Pushed by state law, and public incidents, districts crack down'. *The Enquirer,* Cincinnati [online] 2 March. Accessed 31 March, 2008 from http://news.enquirer.com/apps/pbcs.dll/article?AID=/20080302/NEWS0102/803020345

Lange, Patricia G. (2007a) 'Commenting on Comments: Investigating Responses to Antagonism on YouTube.' Paper presented at *Society for Applied Anthropology Conference*, Tampa, Florida.

— (2007b) 'Publicly private and privately public: Social networking on YouTube.' *Journal of Computer-Mediated Communication*, 13(1): 361–80.

— (2007c) 'The Vulnerable Video Blogger: Promoting Social Change Through Intimacy.' *The Scholar & Feminist Online* 5(2). Available at: http://www.barnard.edu/sfonline/blogs/lange_01.htm

Lanham, Richard A. (2006) *The Economics of Attention: Style and Substance in the Age of Information.* Chicago and London: Chicago University Press.

Latour, Bruno (2005) *Reassembling the Social: An Introduction to Actor-Network-Theory.* Clarendon Lectures in Management Studies. Oxford: Oxford University Press.

Law, John and John Urry (2004) 'Enacting the Social.' *Economy and Society* 33(3): 390–410.

Lee, Ellen (2007) 'Full Cal courses are on YouTube.' *The San Francisco Chronicle*, San Francisco, 4 October. Accessed via Factiva database.

Lee, Richard E. (2007) 'Cultural Studies, Complexity Studies and the Transformation of the Structures of Knowledge.' *International Journal of Cultural Studies* 10(1): 11–20.

Letzing, John (2007) 'UPDATE: Google Unveils Copyright Protection Tools For YouTube.' *Dow Jones Business News,* 16 October. Accessed via Factiva database.

Levy, Pierre (1997) *Collective Intelligence: Mankind's Emerging World in Cyberspace.* Cambridge: Perseus Books.

Li, Kenneth (2006) 'Viacom asks YouTube to purge certain clips.' *Reuters News,* 31 October. Accessed via Factiva database.

Livingstone, Sonia (2004) 'Media Literacy and the Challenge of New Information and Communication Technologies.' *The Communication Review* 7, pp. 3–14.

Lloyd, Annemaree (2007) "Guarding Against Collective Amnesia? Making Significance Problematic: An Exploration of Issues." *Library Trends* 56(1): 53–66.

Lotman, Yuri (1990) *The Universe of the Mind: A Semiotic Theory of Culture.* Bloomington: Indiana University Press; London: I. B. Tauris.

Lotz, Amanda D. (2007) *The Television Will be Revolutionized.* New York and London: New York University Press.

McCracken, Grant (1998). 'The Politics of Plenitude.' *Reason.* August/September. Available at: http://www.reason.com/news/show/30733.html

McKee, Alan (2004) *The Public Sphere: An Introduction.* Cambridge: Cambridge University Press.

McKenna, Barrie (2006) 'At YouTube, a Copyright Conundrum Continues.' *The Globe and Mail*, Canada, October 11, p. B1.

McMurria, John (2006) 'The YouTube Community.' *Flow TV.* 20 October. Available at: http://flowtv.org/?p=48

McRobbie, Angela and Sarah Thornton (2002) 'Rethinking 'Moral Panic' for Multi-Mediated Social Worlds.' *Youth Justice: Critical Readings.* Eds John Muncie and Eugene Mclaughlin. London: Sage, pp. 68–79.

McRobbie, Angela and Jenny Garber (1976) 'Girls and Subcultures.' *Resistance Through Rituals: Youth Subcultures in Post-War Britain.* Eds Stuart Hall and Tony Jefferson. London: HarperCollins, pp. 209–29.

McPherson, Tara (2008) 'A Rule Set for the Future.' *Digital Youth, Innovation, and the Unexpected.* Ed. Tara McPherson. Cambridge, MA: The MIT Press, pp. 1–26.

Madden, Mary (2007) *Online Video.* Pew Internet & American Life Project. 25 July. Available at: http://www.pewinternet.org/PPF/r/219/report_display.asp

Martinson, Jane (2006) 'Google faces copyright fight over YouTube.' *The Guardian*, London, 13 October, p. 30.

Matthews, Mark (2008) 'Science and Innovation Policy and the New (and Old) Economics of Creativity.' *FEAST-CCi Workshop on Creative Destruction: Lessons for Science and Innovation Policy from the Rise of the Creative Industries*, Brisbane, 27 and 28 March.

Matthews, Nicole (2007) 'Confessions to a New Public: Video Nation Shorts.' *Media, Culture & Society* 29(3): 435–48.

Meikle, Graham (2002) *Future Active: Media Activism and the Internet.* Sydney: Pluto Press.

Mensel, Robert E. (1991) 'Kodakers Lying in Wait: Amateur Photography and the Right of Privacy in New York, 1885–1915.' *Arts Quarterly* 1(43): 24–45.

Miles, Adrian (2006) 'A Vision for Genuine Media-Rich Blogging.' *Uses of Blogs*. Eds Axel Bruns and Joanne Jacobs. New York: Peter Lang, pp. 213–22.

Mills, Eleanor (2007) 'Viacom Sued Over Colbert Parody on YouTube.' *ZDNet*. 22 March. Available at: http://news.zdnet.com/2100-9595-6169765.html

Milstein, Dana (2007) 'Case Study: Anime Music Videos.' *Music, Sound and Multimedia: From the Live to the Virtual*. Ed. Jamie Sexton. Edinburgh: Edinburgh University Press, pp. 29–50.

Mittel, Jason (2006) 'Narrative Complexity in Contemporary American Television.' *The Velvet Light Trap* 58, pp. 29–40.

Morrissey, Brian (2006) 'Old Media Faces a Hard Lesson On Sharing.' *Adweek*, 3 April.

Mulhern, Francis (2000) *Culture/Metaculture*. London: Routledge.

Murdock, Graham and Robin McCron, (1976) "Youth and Class: The Career of a Confusion." Eds Geoff Mungham and Geoff Pearson, *Working Class Youth Culture*. London: Routledge and Kegan Paul, pp. 10–26

Murphy, Candace (2006) 'Today's kids have their own outlets for creativity.' *The Oakland Tribune*, 22 July. Accessed via Factiva database.

Murray, Simone (2004) '"Celebrating the Story the Way it Is": Cultural Studies, Corporate Media and the Contested Utility of Fandom.' *Continuum: Journal of Media & Cultural Studies* 1(18): 7–25.

Noguchi, Yuke and Sara Kehaulani Goo (2006) 'To the Media, YouTube Is a Threat and a Tool.' *The Washington Post*, 31 October. Accessed via Factiva database.

Nead, Lynda (2004) 'Animating the Everyday: London on Camera Circa 1900.' *Journal of British Studies* 1(43): 65–90.

Nightingale, Virginia (2007) 'The Cameraphone and Online Image Sharing.' *Continuum: Journal of Media & Cultural Studies* 21(2): 289–301.

Nussenbaum, Evelyn, Oliver Ryan, and Peter Lewis (2005) 'Media on the Cutting Edge.' *Fortune*, 28 November, p. 217.

OECD (2007) 'Participative Web: User-Created Content.' *Working Party on the Information Economy*. Available at: http://www.oecd.org/dataoecd/57/14/38393115.pdf

O'Brien, Damien and Brian Fitzgerald (2006) 'Digital Copyright Law in a YouTube World.' *Internet Law Bulletin* 9(6 and 7): 71–4.

O'Reilly, Tim (2005) 'What is Web 2.0? Design Patterns and Business Models for the Next Generation of Software.' *O'Reilly Network*. Available at: http://www.oreillynet.com/pub/a/oreilly/tim/news/2005/09/30/what-is-web-20.html

Ormerod, Paul (2001) *Butterfly Economics: A New General Theory of Social and Economic Behavior*. New York: Basic Books.

OpenNet Initiative (2008) 'YouTube and the Rise of Geolocational Filtering,' *OpenNet Initiative Blog*, 13 March. Available at: http://opennet.net/blog/?p=232

Paolillo, John C. (2008) 'Structure and Network in the YouTube Core.' Paper presented at *41st Hawaii International Conference on System Sciences*.

Patchin, Justin W. and Sameer Hinduja (2006) 'Bullies Move Beyond the Schoolyard: A Preliminary Look At Cyberbullying.' *Youth Violence and Juvenile Justice* 4(2): 148–69.

Petrik, Paula (1992). 'The Youngest Fourth Estate: The Novelty Toy Printing Press and Adolescence, 1970–1886.' *Small Worlds: Children and Adolescents in America, 1850–1950.* Eds Elliot West and Paula Petrik. Kansas City: University of Kansas Press.

Popper, Karl (1972) *Objective Knowledge.* Oxford: Oxford University Press.

Potts, Jason, Stuart Cunningham, John Hartley, and Paul Ormerod (2008a) 'Social Network Markets: A New Definition of the Creative Industries.' *Journal of Cultural Economics* 32(3): 167–85.

Potts, Jason, John Hartley, John Banks, Jean Burgess, Rachel Cobcroft, Stuart Cunningham, and Lucy Montgomery (2008b), 'Consumer Co-Creation and Situated Creativity.' *Industry & Innovation* 15(5): 459–74.

Prelinger, Rick (2007) 'Archives and Access in the 21st Century.' *Cinema Journal* 46(3): 114–18.

Prensky, Marc (2001a) 'Digital Natives, Digital Immigrants.' *On the Horizon* 9(5).

— (2001b) 'Digital Natives, Digital Immigrants.' *On the Horizon* 9(6).

Quittner, Josh (2006) 'The Flickr Founders: Picturing the Web's Future.' *TIME.* Available at: http://www.time.com/time/magazine/article/0,9171,1186931,00.html

Ramadge, Andrew (2008) 'Why Party Boy Corey is a Genius.' *News.com. au.* Available at: http://www.news.com.au/story/0,23599,23066396-5015729,00.html

Rawstorne, Tom and Brad Crouch (2006) 'The Free-for-All Called YouTube.' *The Sunday Mail*, Australia, 15 October. Accessed via Factiva database.

Rennie, Ellie (2006) *Community Media: A Global Introduction.* Lanham: Rowman & Littlefield.

Rose, Richard (2005) 'Language, Soft Power and Asymmetrical Internet Communication.' *Oxford Internet Institute Research Report No. 7.* Available at: http://www.oii.ox.ac.uk/research/project.cfm?id=7

Ross, Andrew (1991). *Strange Weather: Culture, Science, and Technology in the Age of Limits.* London: Verso.

— (2000) 'The Mental Labor Problem.' *Social Text* 2(18): 1–31.

Rowan, David (2005) 'The Next Big Thing: Video-Sharing Websites; Trendsurfing.' *The Times,* London, 19 November, Magazine, p. 14.

Ryan, Oliver (2006) 'Don't Touch That Dial.' *Fortune* 154(5): 76–7.

Schilt, Kristen (2003) '"A Little Too Ironic": The Appropriation and Packaging of Riot Grrrl Politics By Mainstream Female Musicians.' *Popular Music and Society* 26(10): 5–16.

Schonfield, Erick (2008) 'Is YouTube Building Market Dominance at the Expense of Building a Business?' *Tech Crunch.* Available at: http://www.techcrunch.com/2008/05/30/is-youtube-building-market-dominance-at-the-expense-of-building-a-business/

Segev, Elad, Niv Ahituv, and Karine Barzilai-Nahon (2007) 'Mapping Diversities and Tracing Trends of Cultural Homogeneity/Heterogeneity in Cyberspace.' *Journal of Computer-Mediated Communication* 12(12): 69–97.

Seiberling, Grace and Carolyn Bloore (1986) *Amateurs, Photography, and the Mid-Victorian Imagination.* Chicago: University of Chicago Press.

Shah, Chirag and Gary Marchionini (2007) 'Preserving 2008 Us Presidential Election Videos.' Paper presented at *IWAW'07*, Vancouver, British Columbia, Canada.

Shapiro, Laura (2006). 'You Can't Stop the Signal.' *LiveJournal,* 4 December. http://community.livejournal.com/vidding/893694.html

Shefrin, Elana (2004) '*Lord of the Rings, Star Wars,* and Participatory Fandom: Mapping New Congruences Between the Internet and Media Entertainment Culture.' *Critical Studies in Media Communication* 21(3): 261–81.

Shirky, Clay (2008) *Here Comes Everybody: The Power of Organizing Without Organizations.* New York: Penguin.

Sirius, R. U. (1997) 'Web (VS) TV.' *The Web Magazine,* September, pp. 34–40.

Slonje, Rober and Peter K. Smith (2008) 'Cyberbullying: Another main type of bullying?' *Scandinavian Journal of Psychology* 49 (2): 147–54.

Smith, Bridie (2007) 'Schools Ban YouTube Sites in Cyber-Bully Fight.' *The Age,* Melbourne. 2 March. Available at: http://www.theage.com.au/

Sonesson, Göran (2002) 'The Culture of Modernism: From Transgressions of Art to Arts of Transgression.' *Visio*; 3(3), *Modernism,* pp. 9–26.

Springhall, John (1999) *Youth, Popular Culture and Moral Panics: Penny Gaffs to Gangsta Rap, 1830–1997.* London: Palgrave Macmillan.

Spurgeon, Christina (2008) *Advertising and New Media.* London and New York: Routledge.

Stein, Joel (2006) 'Straight Outta Narnia.' *Time* 167(17): 69.

Stevenson, Nick (2003a) *Cultural Citizenship: Cosmopolitan Questions.* Maidenhead: Open University Press.

— (2003b) 'Cultural Citizenship in the "Cultural" Society: A Cosmopolitan Approach.' *Citizenship Studies* 3(7): 331–48.

Stone, Brad (2007), 'Young Turn to Web Sites Without Rules.' *New York Times*, 02 Jan. Available at: http://www.nytimes.com/2007/01/02/technology/02net.htm.

Storey, John (2003) *Inventing Popular Culture: From Folklore to Globalization*. Malden, MA and Oxford: Blackwell.

Street, Brian (1984) *Literacy in Theory and Practice*. Cambridge: Cambridge University Press.

Swartz, Jon (2007) 'YouTube Gets Media Providers' Help Foiling Piracy.' *USA Today*, 16 October, p. B4.

Tacchi, Jo, Greg Hearn, and Abe Ninan (2004). 'Ethnographic Action Research: A Method for Implementing and Evaluating New Media Technologies. *Information and Communication Technology: Recasting Development*. Ed. K. Prasad. Delhi: BR Publishing Corporation.

Terranova, Tiziana (2000) 'Free Labor: Producing Culture for the Digital Economy.' *Social Text* 2(18): 33–58.

Thompson, John B. (2005) 'The New Visibility.' *Theory, Culture & Society* 22(6): 31–51.

Tracey, Michael (1998) *The Decline and Fall of Public Service Broadcasting*. Oxford, New York: Oxford University Press.

TubeMogul (2007) 'What Counts as a View? "View" Testing for Various Online Video Sites.' *TubeMogul.com*. Available at: http://www.tubemogul.com/research/video_views_study.php

Turner, Fred (2006) *From Counterculture to Cyberculture: Steward Brand, the Whole Earth Network and the Rise of Digital Utopianism*. Chicago: Chicago University Press.

Turner, Graeme (2004) *Understanding Celebrity*. London: Sage.

— (2006) 'The Mass Production of Celebrity: "Celetoids", Reality TV and the "Demotic Turn".' *International Journal of Cultural Studies* 2(9): 153–66.

Uricchio, William (2004) 'Cultural Citizenship in the Age of P2P Networks.' In *European Culture and the Media*. Eds Ib Bondebjerg and Peter Golding. Bristol: Intellect Books, pp. 139–63.

Veiga, Alex (2006) 'Anti-Piracy System Could Hurt YouTube.' *Associated Press Newswires*, 13 October. Accessed via Factiva database.

Von Hippel, Eric (2005) *Democratizing Innovation*. Cambridge, MA: The MIT Press.

Wallenstein, Andrew (2006a) 'Biz not sure how to treat upstart YouTube.' *The Hollywood Reporter*, 21 March. Available at: http://www.hollywoodreporter.com/hr/search/article_display.jsp?vnu_content_id=1002199881

— (2006b) 'MTV2 embraces embattered YouTube video-sharing site.' *Reuters News*, 3 March. Accessed via Factiva database.

Warschauer, Mark (2003) *Technology and Social Inclusion: Rethinking the Digital Divide*. Cambridge, Massachusetts: MIT Press.

Weinberger, David (2007) *Everything is Miscellaneous: The Power of the New Digital Disorder*. New York: Times Books.

Williams, Raymond (1958) 'Culture is Ordinary.' *Resources of Hope. Culture, Democracy, Socialism*. Ed. Robin Gable (1989). London: Verso, pp. 3–18.

Zimmermann, Patricia (1995) *Reel Families: A Social History of Amateur Film*. Bloomington: Indiana University Press.

Zittrain, Jonathan (2008) *The Future of the Internet and How to Stop It*. New Haven: Yale University Press.

Index